LINGUISTIC MINORITIES IN MULTILINGUAL SETTINGS

STUDIES IN BILINGUALISM (SiBil)

EDITORS

KEES DE BOT
University of Nijmegen

THOM HUEBNER
San José State University

EDITORIAL BOARD

Michael Clyne *(Monash University)*
Theo van Els *(University of Nijmegen)*
Charles Ferguson *(Stanford University)*
Joshua Fishman *(Yeshiva University)*
François Grosjean *(Université de Neuchâtel)*
Wolfgang Klein *(Max Planck Institut für Psycholinguistik)*
Christina Bratt Paulston *(University of Pittsburgh)*
Suzanne Romaine *(Merton College, Oxford)*
Charlene Sato *(University of Hawaii at Manoa)*
Merrill Swain *(Ontario Institute for Studies in Education)*
Richard Tucker *(Carnegie Mellon University)*

Volume 4

Christina Bratt Paulston

Linguistic Minorities in Multilingual Settings

LINGUISTIC MINORITIES IN MULTILINGUAL SETTINGS

IMPLICATIONS FOR LANGUAGE POLICIES

CHRISTINA BRATT PAULSTON
University of Pittsburgh

JOHN BENJAMINS PUBLISHING COMPANY
AMSTERDAM/PHILADELPHIA

1994

The paper used in this publication meets the minimum requirements of American National Standard for Information Sciences — Permanence of Paper for Printed Library Materials, ANSI Z39.48-1984.

Library of Congress Cataloging-in-Publication Data

Paulston, Christina Bratt, 1932-
   Linguistic minorities in multilingual settings : implications for language policies / Christina Bratt Paulston.
     p.   cm. -- (Studies in bilingualism, ISSN 0928-1533 ; v. 4)
   Includes bibliographical references (p.).
   1. Multilingualism. 2. Language policy. 3. Linguistic minorities. I. Title. II. Series: Studies in bilingualism ; vol. 4.
P115.P38   1994
306.4'46--dc20   93-44796
ISBN 90 272 4104 X (Eur.)/1-55619-347-5 (US) (Hb; alk. paper)   CIP
ISBN 90 272 4112 0 (Eur.)/1-55619-540-0 (US) (Pb; alk. paper)

© Copyright 1994 - John Benjamins B.V.
No part of this book may be reproduced in any form, by print, photoprint, microfilm, or any other means, without written permission from the publisher.

John Benjamins Publishing Co. · P.O. Box 75577 · 1070 AN Amsterdam · The Netherlands
John Benjamins North America · 821 Bethlehem Pike · Philadelphia, PA 19118 · USA

*For Christopher-Rolland and Ian Rollandsson
and, as always, Rolland*

Contents

Preface   ix

PART I

Chapter 1   3
Multilingualism and Language Policies

Chapter 2   9
Social Factors in Language Maintenance and Language Shift

Chapter 3   25
Ethnicity and Nationalism

PART II

Introduction   43

Chapter 4   47
Catalan and Occitan: Comparative Test Cases for a Theory of Language Maintenance and Shift

Chapter 5   59
Case Studies: Tanzania, Peru, Sweden

Chapter 6   79
Language Revitalization: The Case of Irish

Chapter 7   91
Language Regenesis: Language Revival, Revitalization and Reversal

Chapter 8 Epilogue	107
Notes	111
Bibliography	115
Author Index	131
Subject Index	135

Preface

Some books more or less write themselves. This one certainly didn't.

The background to this book, which has been some 14 years in the writing, was initially an unsuccessful attempt to explain language maintenance. I have long thought that research failures, preferably others', are informative and helpful in considering your own research, but such accounts are hard to come by. I will begin therefore with a retelling of my field work in Catalunya, Spain, which eventually lead to the present conceptualization.

In 1978 I wrote a research proposal in which I intended to study Catalan language maintenance:

> In spite of prolonged and severe pressure over centuries by central authorities to impose the sole use of Castilian Spanish in Catalonia, Catalan remains a viable language (with about eight million speakers), which only a few months ago was recognized as an official language in post-Franco Spain. Just why has Catalan endured over the centuries (Rossinyol, 1974) when so many other ethnic groups have shifted to the dominant language of their nation. Why has Catalan reached official status while the closely related Occitan (spoken in southern France) can be considered an "endangered language" (Kirsch, 1977)? This project addresses the problems of ethnic groups and their persistence with the focus on language maintenance as a function of ethnic boundary maintenance (Barth, 1969), using Catalan as a case study.
>
> Catalonia neatly exemplifies Barth's point that boundaries between ethnic groups persist in spite of a flow of personnel between them, in spite of stable interaction across boundaries, and in this study Catalan will not be considered as a cause of ethnic cohesion but rather as a resultant mechanism for ethnic persistence.

An acceptable enough proposal except that the theoretical framework turned out to be not acceptable, i.e. it was an inappropriate conceptualization on my part. It took me several months in the field to come to this reluctant conclusion. First, the reaction of Catalan officials to dialect features struck me as very atypical; they were perfectly willing to accept any variant dialect as standard Catalan, very different reactions from my previous experience with ethnic languages. Second, I found the criterion for group membership very fluid. Typically, ethnicity is based on a shared biological past (whether fictitiously or not). One informant, whose Turkish Jewish parents had moved to Barcelona, declared categorically: "Sure, I am Catalana, I grew up in Barcelona." By contrast, growing up in Watts or Eastern Los Angeles is not going to turn anyone into Black or Chicano. Finally, in December of 1978 there was a public debate whether anyone who had lived five years in Barcelona should officially become Catalan. That is not ethnic group boundary maintenance as I know it. So I withdrew my original conceptualization and searched for another until I eventually settled on geographic nationalism and developed the theoretical framework presented here.

The theoretical model is grounded on a wide variety of data: my own fieldwork data and school visits on five continents, as well as just living overseas (Morocco, India, Peru, Sweden and Spain), teaching courses on language planning and directing dissertations on language shift and spread, as well as the examination of numerous case studies of social, political, and religious groups in multilingual situations. My students often ask me how you know when you have enough data. My answer is when you get no new information or find any exceptions to your model. I am reasonably satisfied that language maintenance and shift can be usefully examined and educational language policies understood and analyzed from the perspective mentioned here.

Of some chapters, earlier versions were published previously, and I would like to thank the publishers for granting me permission to use this material: and earlier version of Chapter 2 appeared in *The Fergusonian Impact* Vol. 2, ed. by J.A. Fishman (Mouton de Gruyter, Berlin,

1986); of Chapter 3 in *Multicultural Education* (Organization for Economic Cooperation and Development, Paris, 1987); of Chapter 4 in *International Journal of the Sociology of Language*, Vol. 63, 1987 (Mouton de Gruyter); and of Chapter 7 in *Journal of Multilingual and Multicultural Development*, Dec. 1993 (Multilingual Matters).

No scholar works in a vacuum, and the bibliography is one manifestation of my many debts to other scholars. I here acknowledge with gratitude the stimulation and help I have received from my colleagues over the years — you will surely know who you are. I am also grateful to Professor Richard Cottam who allowed me to follow his course on nationalism and who introduced me to its vast literature. Kees de Bot was an informed and thoughtful editor, and the book is much improved by his advice. And this brief statement of acknowledgement would be sorely incomplete without the recognition of the role my students have taken in the shaping of the theoretical framework with their many astute questions, their counter examples and their own case studies. Thanks go especially to Mary C. Connerty and Pow Chee Chen who helped write the "Language Regenesis" chapter.

Pittsburgh 1993

PART I

Chapter 1

Multilingualism and Language Policies

Introduction

Most nations in the world are multilingual, i.e. they contain ethnic groups in contact and not infrequently in competition. The major language problems which face the policy makers of such nation states are choice of national or official language(s), choice of alphabet, and choice of medium of instruction. People have rioted and faced death over unpopular choices, frequently in defense of their own language but not necessarily so. The 1976 Soweto riots in South Africa concerned a change of medium of instruction in the schools from English to Afrikaans neither of which language was native to the students. At other times there have been peaceful implementation and acceptance of national languages which are not native to the various ethnic groups. Tanzania is one of the very few African ex-colonies which has an indigenous African language as a national language, and although Swahili is native to a very small group, it has peacefully and successfully become implemented and accepted as the national language in contrast to Swahili in neighboring Kenya which still uses English. In Singapore, the clear preference of the Chinese for their children is instruction in English.

What generalizations can we make about language policies in multilingual states and how can we predict success and failure? We know that the major possible linguistic outcomes of the prolonged contact of ethnic groups are basically three: language maintenance, bilingualism, or language shift. Bilingualism may also involve the spread of a lingua franca, an LWC (language of wider communication). An understanding of language maintenance and shift and the social conditions under which they occur constitutes a major means for understanding language policies which seek to regulate the interactions of ethnic groups within a modern nation-state. No language policy will be successful which goes counter to existing sociocultural forces. The difficulty lies in understanding and identifying which are the relevant social determinants of maintenance and shift.

We have at present a very poor understanding of which social variables are germane to ethnic group relations and their consequences, and in this book I would like to explore some possibilities of understanding. I will do so in a comparative approach of case studies and will draw on a wide variety of data: my own fieldwork data and school visits on five continents; impressions and observations from my own work with training teachers from ethnic groups and directing doctoral dissertations on language shift and spread; and examination of numerous case studies of social and political groups in multilingual situations.

I will here present an analytical framework for explaining and predicting the language behavior of social groups as such behavior relates to linguistic policies for minority groups. I argue a number of points: (1) if language planning is to be successful, it must consider the social context of language problems and especially the forces which contribute to language maintenance or shift; (2) the linguistic consequences for social groups in contact will vary depending on the focus of social mobilization, i.e. ethnicity or nationalism; (3) a major problem in the accurate prediction of such linguistic consequences lies in identifying the salient factors which contribute to language maintenance or shift, i.e. answering the question "under what conditions." Rational policy-making requires that all these factors be considered in the establishment and understanding of educational policies for minority groups.

Language Planning and Language Problems

Most scholars limit the term language planning to "the organized pursuit of solutions to language problems, typically at the national level" (Fishman, 1973:23-24). The degree of "organized" varies; a language planning process which shares Jernudd's specification of the orderly and systematic (a) establishment of goals, (b) selection of means, and (c) prediction of outcomes (Jernudd, 1973:11-23) is an exception rather than the rule. Heath makes clear in her study of language policy in Mexico (1972) that language decisions are primarily made on political and economic grounds and reflect the value of those in political power. Linguistic issues *per se* are of minor concern. Since the matters discussed are overtly those of language, there is frequently confusion about the salient issues discussed in language planning, whether they are, in fact, matters of political, economic, religious, sociocultural or linguistic concern, or even moral concern. OECD's (Organization for Economic Co-operation and Development) longstanding interest in the educational policies for minority social groups serves to emphasize the legitimate and important economic implications such language policies have; one can even argue that the most important factor influencing language choice of ethnic groups is economic, specifically one of access to jobs (Brudner, 1972).

Language choice is one of the major language problems, whether it be choice of national language (as in Finland and Israel), choice of national alphabet (as in Albania and Somalia), or choice of medium of instruction (as in Norway). In Israel, social conditions and religious attitudes towards Hebrew and the Promised Land made possible the rebirth of Hebrew and its implementation as a national language. "As to the success of the Hebrew revival, it was probably due largely to the prevalence of the required conditions" (Nahir, 1984:302); that is, Israel serves as an example of social forces facilitating national language planning. In contrast, Peru during the Velasco government officialized Quechua as a national language (Mannheim, 1984) with resounding failure of implementation. In Peru, as in much of Latin America, race is defined primarily by cultural attributes: wear a long braid, and many faldas, wide Indian type skirts, and speak Quechua and you are Indian; cut your hair, wear European style clothing and speak Spanish, and you become if not white, at least mestizo (Patch, 1967). To embrace Quechua would be to declare oneself Indian with all the accompanying socioeconomic stigmatization, and such planning held no hope of successful implementation. Peru serves as an example of language planning which goes counter to existing socio-cultural forces.

The problem is of course to be able to identify relevant social forces and predict the outcomes they will have. For example, contrary to expectation, choice of medium of instruction in the schools, especially for minority groups,[1] has very little predictive power in the final language choice of the ethnic group. The difficulty is that we have a very poor grasp of what the relevant social forces are and what the corresponding educational, social, and cultural outcomes will be. Three points need to be made here. The major point to understand about language as group behavior[2] is that language is almost never the causal factor, never the factor that gives rise to, brings about, and causes things to happen, but rather language mirrors social conditions, mirrors man's relationship to man. It is quite true that denying African Americans access to schooling as was common in the U.S. South in the last century made them unfit for anything but menial jobs, but Black illiteracy was not the cause of Black/White relations and exploitation, it was the result of it.

The corollary to this simple, yet hard to grasp point is that bilingual education (mother tongue education, home language education, i.e. education in the national language plus the ethnic group's own language) is in itself not a causal factor. One reason there is no conclusive answer in the research on bilingual education of the seemingly simple question of whether a child learns to read more rapidly in a second language if first taught to read in his primary (Engle, 1975:1) is that medium of instruction in school programs is an intervening variable rather than the independent variable it is always treated as. One cannot hope to achieve any consensus in research findings by examining intervening variables without identifying the independent variables (Paulston, 1975). Schools and schooling can facilitate existing social trends, but they cannot be successful counter to social and economic forces. English medium schools were the major language learning facility for the children of the European immigrants to the United States, but the same schools have not been successful in teaching English to Navajo children on the reservations and they have had their fair share of failure in Chicano education. "Under what social conditions does medium of instruction make a difference for school children in achieving success?" remains one key question.

The third point relates to the possible linguistic outcomes of the prolonged contact of ethnic groups within one nation, the typical background situation which necessitates special educational policies for minority groups. There are not many possibilities: the three main ones are language maintenance, bilingualism, or language shift. Other possibilities are language convergence and the creation of pidgins and creoles but they entail bilingualism or shift and will not be further considered.

For an overview of the range of language problems and their intended treatments, see Nahir's "Language Planning Goals: A Classification" (1984). The eleven goals he mentions are (1) language purification, (2) language revival, (3) language reform, (4) language standardization, (5) language spread, (6) lexical modernization, (7) terminology unification, (8) stylistic simplification, (9) interlingual communication, (10) language maintenance, and (11) auxiliary-code standardization.

There is no doubt at all that multilingual states often face language problems or, put more cautionary, problems which involve languages. There is always a legitimate question whether these same problems would exist under different social and economic situations, would exist in an expanding economy, under a social democracy, etc. Another question is whether language planning and policies can have any effect on these problems. Everyone's favorite case study of language planning, the revival of Hebrew, seems just to have happened without any formal planning; what brought Hebrew "alive was achieved by glorious improvisation" (Glinert, 1991:221). These issues of language problems and language policies are concerns I here undertake to explore.

Chapter 2

Social Factors in Language Maintenance and Language Shift

Introduction

In this chapter I wish to present some generalizations about social conditions which support language maintenance or shift, formed in my efforts of a better understanding of bilingual education. The main point is simply that ethnic groups within a modern nation-state, given opportunity and incentive, typically shift to the language of the dominant group. It is not likely to be a popular view, but the implications are so important for the implementation of language policies that I think we must face what is, not what we wish to be.

To the study of language maintenance and shift, we need to add two other related topics, language spread (Cooper, 1982) and language death (Dorian, 1981; Dressler and Wodak-Leodolter, 1977; Hindley, 1990). Cooper defines language spread as "an increase, over time, in the proportion of a communication network that adopts a given language or language variety for a given communicative function" (1982:6). Most language spread probably takes place as lingua francas, as LWC's (languages of wider communication), and English is a good example (Fishman, Cooper, and Conrad, 1977). On the whole, such spread is neutral in attitudes.

But languages also spread for purposes of within-nation communication, and when they do so, not as an additional language like

English in Nigeria, but as a new mother tongue, then language spread becomes a case of language shift. When such language spread through shift takes place within groups who do not possess another territorial base, we have a case of language death. Languages do become extinct, and the many dead Amerindian languages are now a mute witness to the spread of English (Bauman, 1980). Language shift, especially if it involves language death, tends to be an emotional topic; and economists and other social scientists who are not basically interested in language and culture *per se* will simply have to accept that it is often fairly futile to insist on a reasoned view on matters of language shift where it concerns the opinions and attitudes of the speakers of the shifting groups. Linguists and anthropologists frequently belong in this category as well.

In addition, the data base is very small. For example, in Gal's fine dissertation (1979) on language shift in bilingual Austria, the ten page bibliography contains only *six* entries which mention shift or maintenance in the title. I know of no major study on language maintenance, presumably because it is not considered problematic (but see Fase, Jaspaert & Kroon, 1992), except as anthropologists study cultural retention (see Spicer, 1980; Castile and Kushner, 1981).

Origin of the contact situation

One of the primary factors in accounting for subsequent course of mother tongue diversity, to use Lieberson's phrase, lies in the origin of the contact situation (Lieberson, Dalto, and Johnston, 1975; Schermerhorn, 1970). Voluntary migration, especially of individuals and families, results in the most rapid shift; annexation and colonialization where entire groups are brought into a nation with their social institutions of marriage and kinship, religious and other belief and value systems still *in situ*, still more or less intact, tend to result in much slower language shift if at all. Lieberson et al. claim "that the course of race and ethnic relations will be different in settings where the subordinate group is indigenous as opposed to those where the migrant populations are subordinate" (1975:53). They consider four groups: (1) indigenous superordinate, (2) migrant superordinate, (3) indigenous subordinate, and (4) migrant subordinate. They find it unlikely that much, if any, mother-tongue shift will occur among the first two groups. "Almost certainly a group enjoying both political and economic dominance will be in a position to ensure that its linguistic position is maintained. Bilingualism may occur, but this is not the same as mother-tongue shift: At the very most, one can normally expect only an extremely slow rate of mother-tongue change among such groups" (1975:53). The role of Swedish in Finland illustrates that point and gives us an example of an ethnic group in demographic and political decline which uses its native tongue to maintain its boundaries for ethnic survival (R. G. Paulston, 1977), but its continued role in Finland is best explained by the former superordinate status of its mother-tongue speakers. The French in England (after the Battle of Hastings in 1066) is another example of a superordinate minority group who maintained their language for some three hundred years but finally shifted when they lost their mainland territories.

Subordinate groups who are indigenous at the time of contact, either through colonization as in the case of the American Indians or through annexation as in the case of the Chicanos in the U.S. Southwest, are unlikely to change rapidly. Migrant subordinate groups are the only groups likely to show rapid rates of mother-tongue shift, and in the United States, as Lieberson et al. show, the immigrant experience was one of extraordinarily rapid shift. In contrast, within the same nation and with access to the same educational institution of public schooling, the indigenous subordinate groups have changed at a much slower rate. In 1940, 20 percent of the whites in Louisiana still reported French as their mother-tongue, although the state had been purchased almost 150 years before, from France in 1803. In New Mexico, conquered in 1846, nearly 45 percent of the Native Parentage population (third or later generation) reported, also in 1940, Spanish as their mother-tongue, which means that, since a fair proportion of this population was not of Spanish origin, much more than half of the Spanish-speaking population, had not shifted (Lieberson et al., 1975). In contrast to Louisiana, the Southwest has a steady trickle of new immigrants, legal and illegal, from Mexico, and no one really knows the exact rate of language shift, but Thompson (1974) calculates that in Texas Spanish has remained the mother-tongue for eighty percent of the third generation.

The Indian population probably has been the slowest to become bilingual. Lieberson et al. cite census data which show that as recently as 1900 slightly more than 40 percent of the Indian population could not speak English. Many of those who did speak English also maintained their Indian mother tongue, and Lieberson et al. conclude that "it is clear that mother-tongue shift was far slower than for the subordinate immigrant groups" (1975:56).

While such a complicated phenomenon as language maintenance and shift can only be the result of multiple causality, the origin of the contact situation is clearly one of the major social factors in accounting for the subsequent language outcomes.

Factors in language shift

Maintained group bilingualism[3] is unusual, *if* opportunity of access to the dominant language is present and incentives, especially socioeconomic, motivate a shift to the dominant language. If not, as with India's former caste system and ascribed status, the result is language maintenance. But given access and incentive, the norm for groups in prolonged contact within a modern nation-state is for the subordinate group to shift to the language of the dominant group, either over several hundred years as with Gaelic in Great Britain or over the span of three generations as has been the case of the European immigrants to Australia and the United States in a very rapid shift. It was exactly the language shift and attempts to stop it which have caused much of the trouble in Quebec (from French to English [Gendron, 1972]) and Belgium (from Flemish to French [Verdoodt, 1978]).

The mechanism of language shift is bilingualism, often but not necessarily with exogamy, where parent(s) speak(s) the original language with the grandparents and the new language with the children. The case of bilingualism holds in all cases of group shifts, although the rate of shift may vary with several bilingual generations rather than just one.

Language shift frequently begins with women (granted access and incentive), manifest in choice of code (Schlieben-Lange, 1977); in choice of marriage partner (Gal, 1979; Brudner, 1972); and eventually in the language in which they choose to bring up their children (Eckert, 1983). The most common explanation is that women, who are in a subordinate position in society, are sensitive to issues of power, including the language of power, but there really exists no generally accepted explanation.

Language shift is often treated by laymen and social scientists alike as an unarguable indicator of cultural assimilation, and it is often the painful thought of forsaking the culture and values of the forefathers that is at the root of the strife over language shift. Assimilation is a much more complex issue than language shift, but a few points need to be considered. We need here to make the distinction, in Schermerhorn's terms (1970), between social and cultural institutions.

Schermerhorn sees three major causal factors as determining the nature of the relationship between ethnic groups and the process of integration into the environing society. The first refers to the origin of the contact situation between "the subordinate ethnic and dominant groups, such as annexation, migration, and colonization," the second to "the degree of enclosure (institutional separation or segmentation) of the subordinate group or groups from the society-wide network of institutions and associations," and the third to "the degree of control exercised by dominant groups over access to scarce resources by subordinate groups in a given society" (1970:15).

Schermerhorn also posits three intervening or contextual variables which modify the effect of the independent variables. The most important is the agreement or disagreement between dominant and subordinate groups on collective goals for the latter, such as assimilation or pluralism. He bases his discussion on Wirth's typology of the different policies adopted by minority groups in response to their unprivileged position.

> These policies [Wirth] called assimilationist, pluralist, secessionist, and militant. Briefly, assimilationist policy seeks to merge the minority members into the wider society by abandoning their own cultural distinctiveness and adopting their superordinates' values and style of life. The pluralist strategy solicits tolerance from the dominant group that will allow the subordinates to retain much of their cultural distinctiveness. The secessionist minority aims to separate or detach itself from the superordinates so as to pursue an independent existence. Finally, the militants ... intend to gain control over the dominants who currently have the ascendancy (1970:78).

Schermerhorn points out that assimilation and pluralism really refer to cultural aspects while secession and militancy refer to structural ones.

> To clarify this problem it is well to insist on the analytic distinction between culture and social structure. Culture signifies the ways of action learned through socialization, based on norms and values that serve as guides or standards for that behavior. Social structure, on the other hand, refers to "the set of crystallized social relationships

> which its (the society's) members have with each other which places them in groups, large or small, permanent or temporary, formally organized or unorganized, and which relates them to the major institutional activities of the society, such as economic and occupational life, religion, marriage and the family, education, government, and recreation" (Gordon, 1964:30-31), (1970:80).

In order to deal with the difficulty of applying cultural features to conditions which involve social features, he makes the distinction between assimilation, which is cultural, and incorporation, which is socio-structural.

Economic incorporation of an ethnic group with access to the goods and services of a nation is the common goal of minority groups and the most common reason for the recent migration in Europe (some also claim religious freedom or refugee status). Economic incorporation is different from cultural assimilation and the giving up of values and beliefs, but it is primarily to the perception of forced assimilation that the issue of the medium of instruction in the national language becomes tied. Many Chicanos bemoan the loss of Chicano culture with the loss of Spanish, but there is not necessarily an isomorphic relationship between language and culture. Spanish is the carrier of many other cultures besides Chicano, and less commonly accepted by scholars, language maintenance is not necessary for culture and ethnicity maintenance, as indeed Lopez (1978) documents for the Chicanos in Los Angeles. In other words, it is possible for groups to maintain their own ethnic culture even after language shift, as we see in groups like the English gypsies and many AmerIndian tribes.

Although most ethnic minority groups within a nation, given access and incentive, do shift language, they will vary in their degree of ethnic maintenance and in their *rate* of shift. Some causal factors can be identified. For example, in Pittsburgh the Greeks shift over a four generation span compared with the three generation shift of the Italians. Some factors which contribute to the slower Greek shift are (a) knowledge and access to a standardized, written language with cultural prestige and tradition, which is taught by the Greek churches in Pittsburgh, and (b) arranged marriage partners directly from Greece (who are then monolingual in Greek). The Italians in contrast speak/ spoke a non-standard, non-written dialect with no prestige, and they shared their Roman Catholic churches with the English-speaking Irish, typically with Irish priests and nuns, so they found no language maintenance support in the churches. Nor was there any pressure for endogamy as long as the marriage was within the Roman Catholic Church. So we see that important features in supporting prolonged language maintenance are marriage patterns of endogamy, a prestigious language with literary tradition, and access to a social institution with formal instruction, i.e. literacy in the original mother-tongue.

Ethnic groups also vary in, quite vaguely, ethnic pride or ethnic stubbornness in culture maintenance — even after they have shifted language and become socially incorporated into a nation. Alba says in the preface to his book about Catalunya: "Catalonia is not especially notable for anything except its persistence — its stubbornness in existing despite the most adverse conditions" (1975:ii). The survival of Catalan may best be explained as a result of nationalism but it does exemplify the notion of stubbornness, as Alba calls it, in group maintenance.

Groups also vary in group adhesion, and there is wide intra-group variation in members' attitudes toward language maintenance and cultural assimilation. A case in point is Richard Rodriguez' beautiful, autobiographical but controversial *Hunger of Memory* (1982), in which he argues for assimilation — and against bilingual education. Carillo's comments on this work are worth citing:

> Mexican-American children were a minority in the schools. There was a strong pressure to assimilate; the overwhelming presence of the dominant anglo society was enough to cause this pressure. Add to this the impression of a sensitive child that the rewards of the society were limited to those who were members of the dominant culture, and you can begin to understand Rodriguez' conflicting

> feelings about learning English, maintaining his Spanish, assimilating to anglo society, and maintaining his ties to Mexican-American culture.
> Today, growing up Mexican-American in California is very different. As the minority group has grown, it has influenced the dominant culture significantly. ...Today, a Mexican-American child in California has many options on the scale from complete assimilation to strong pride in Mexican-American culture (1984:9, 30).

Carillo does not write as a social scientist but as a participant Chicano and ESL (English as a Second Language) professional, and he documents his perception of social change, in the host culture as well as the minority group, in his defense of the much criticized Rodriguez.[4] Carillo's point about many options available stresses the need for flexible educational policies.

Opportunity of access to the second language (L2) is a necessary condition for language shift. Some general factors of social conditions which influence access to the L2 are:

a) participation in social institutions, primarily universal schooling, exogamy, and required military service, and often religious institutions.
b) access to mass-media, especially TV.
c) access to roads and transportation versus physical isolation, like islands and mountains.
d) travel, including trade, commerce, war, and evangelism.
e) occupations which necessitate or allow social intercourse with native speakers, like busdriver, salesperson, etc..
f) demographic factors, like size of groups, vast in-migration, continued migration, back-migration, urbanization.

The major social institution facilitating L2 learning in a situation which favors language shift is without a doubt public schooling. With children from socially marginal groups like the Navajo Indians (Rosier & Holm, 1980; Spolsky, 1977), bilingual education tends to be the more efficient form of public education, but with children from socially favored groups, education in the national language is a viable alternative, as the literature on the Canadian immersion programs for middle class children attests to (Cohen & Swain, 1976; Lambert & Tucker, 1972; Swain & Lapkin, 1982). There is a vast literature on the pros and cons of bilingual education, and the issues are too complicated to discuss here in any detail (see e.g. Center for Applied Linguistics, 1977; Churchill, 1986; Cummins, 1976; Garcia, 1991; Hartford, Valdman and Foster, 1982; Paulston, 1980, 1988; Spolsky, 1972; Tosi, 1984; Cazden and Snow, 1990; Paulston, 1992; Baker, 1993; Baetens Beardsmore, 1993).

A social institution for adults which can contribute markedly to L2 learning is the Armed Forces. In Peru, military service paired with the necessary travel to the coast district has been the major means of learning Spanish for many Quechua young men, former school drop-outs. In Zaire, during the colonial times of the Belgian Congo, Flemish officers did not insist on French, and the Armed Forces became a major force in the spread of Lingala, a local pidgin LWC, which became the language of the army.

Exogamy, marrying outside the ethnic group or other social unit, typically necessitates language shift for one partner, at least within the family. This shift usually is in the direction of the language of the socio-economically favored group. This is exactly what happened in French Canada (Lieberson, 1970), but the French-speaking Canadians held political power and through legislation have been able to protect the position of French. Language maintenance and shift in regions where political and socio-economic power is divided between the ethnic groups is difficult and probably impossible to predict. Exogamy, showing definite trends of direction, is the most positive indicator of incipient shift.

Data on demographic factors are troublesome. Apart from concerns about reliability and validity of the database (de Vries, 1977; Thompson, 1974) and methods of analysis (see Section II, "Demography" in Mackey and Ornstein, 1979; McConnell, 1992), we do not really know what constitutes a critical mass in language maintenance of an ethnic group. We recognize that maintenance is easier for a large group, but we do not know how large is large. Clearly other factors like elitist status and prestige are at work here as well.

Most of the other factors are self-explanatory although I should point out that there exists no hard quantificational data base, and this list has been collected from a reading of case studies where these conditions are often treated observationally and anecdotally.

We see then that the major linguistic consequence of ethnic groups in prolonged contact within a nation-state is language shift of the subordinate groups to the language of the dominant group. The major dependent variable is the rate of shift. A very slow shift which spans many generations results in a long state of bilingualism which affects the structure of the languages involved (Thomason & Kaufman, 1988), as Spanish expressions in Peru like *no mas* and diminutives like *chiquititito,* which are calqued on Quechua (Albo, 1970; see also Pfaff, 1981). What is less understood and really not studied at all is the degree to which such groups keep their communicative competence rules[5] and apply their own rules of appropriate language use to the new language. An Arab who speaks fluent Swedish but stands as close, touches as much, interrupts as often, etc. as it is appropriate to do in a conversation in Arabic, will have a confusing and probably irritating effect on a Swede who has very different rules for using language. We know virtually nothing about this aspect of language shift, but it is easy to speculate that a slow shift is more likely to guard cultural ways of using language, and we know that different standards for using language (like appropriate loudness of voice) easily become a source of friction between groups. This topic merits study because the different communicative competence rules show up clearly in the classroom (Philips, 1970), and the children suffer as a consequence, since the teacher's rules are always held to be the "right" ones.

But this shift only takes place if there are opportunity and incentive for the group to learn the national language. There are probably many kinds of incentives (the database here is very inadequate) but the two major ones are (1) economic advantage, primarily in the form of source of income, and (2) social prestige. In Brudner's terms (1972), jobs select language learning strategies, which is to say, wherever there are jobs available that demand knowledge of a certain language, people will learn it. Without rewards, language learning is not salient. Sometimes language shift is held to be problematic (Quebec), sometimes it is encouraged as national policy (France), sometimes it is resisted by the ethnic group (Catalan) and sometimes encouraged (European immigrants to Australia and the United States), but it is invariable to the social conditions that one must look to understand the attitudes and values which accompany language shift.

Factors in language maintenance

Where shift does not take place, it is for three major reasons:

a. Self-imposed boundary maintenance (Barth, 1969), always for reasons other than language, most frequently religion, e.g. the Amish and the orthodox Jewish Hassidim. The Hassidim are perfectly aware of the role of English but their choice is for group cohesion for religious purposes:

> Many [Lubovitch] families elect to send their children to the Yiddish speaking school [no English curriculum]. In so doing, they increase the possibility of upward mobility within the ethnic group and decrease the probability that these children will gain the secular and technical skills necessary for employment in the economy of the larger society. All Lubovitchers are aware of the potential usefulness of secular skills and an English curriculum, but few ... families elect the bilingual school for their children (Levy, 1975:40).

Such extreme measures of language maintenance are very unusual and never undertaken over time only for the sake of language itself.

b. Externally imposed boundaries (cf. Schermerhorn's degree of enclosure), usually in the form of denied access to goods and services, especially jobs. The African American community of the past in the U.S. is an example. Geographic isolation (which is theoretically uninteresting but nevertheless effective) is also a form of external boundary which contributes to language maintenance, as Gaelic in the Hebrides or Quechua in the Andes.

c. A diglossic-like (Ferguson, 1959; 1991) situation where the two languages exist in a situation of functional distribution where each language has its specified purpose and domain, and the one language is inappropriate in the other situation, as with Guarani and Spanish in Paraguay (Rubin, 1968), or with Modern Standard Arabic and the mother tongues in the Maghreb (Grandguillaume, 1983).

The third consequence is prolonged group bilingualism. This is not the place for a thorough discussion on the nature of bilingualism (Albert and Obler, 1978; Baker, 1993; Cummins and Swain, 1986; Grosjean, 1982; Hamers and Blanc, 1989; Hornby, 1977; Lambert, 1972; Mackey, 1976; Miracle, 1983; Romaine, 1989), but it should be mentioned that full-fledged, balanced bilingualism is the exception rather than the rule. Bilingualism spans a range from passive, imperfect knowledge of dead sacred languages (Sanskrit, classical Arabic, classical Hebrew, Suryoyo, etc.) to the linguistic competence necessary for simultaneous interpretation. Degree of proficiency has little to do with language attitudes, and the sacred languages particularly assert a vast influence on attempts to orderly language planning.

Another perspective from which to consider language maintenance is that of language as a social resource, similar to religion.

Language can be seen as a resource which is available to ethnic groups in their competition for access to the goods and services of a nation. All groups do not avail themselves of language as a symbol in their fight for independence or economic shares or for whatever goal they see as in their best interest. When they do, language can be a very effective power base, as the nationalistic movements in Europe in the last century bear witness to. Language loyalty was so often romanticized during these movements that one does well to remember that there is nothing inherently "natural" about group language loyalty, but rather that it is a deliberately chosen strategy for survival.

Mohammed Kabir documents these points in his dissertation on "Changing Faces of Nationalism in Bangladesh" (1985). His claim is that the economy is the crucial factor in bringing about change in a nation, and as change occurs, so do members' loyalties and their bases therefore. Members choose political identity and mobilize along particular strategies depending on their particular demands. So language, ethnicity, and religion are available resources and are chosen as identity bases variously over time as strategies to achieve specific demands.

Bengal, Kabir's case study, was populated by the same ethnolinguistic group, roughly half of whom were Muslim and the other half Hindu. Eventually the Hindu group came to dominate education and agriculture. In 1905 Bengal was split into East and West Bengal against the opposition of the Hindus, and in 1912 Bengal was reunited, this time against the will of the Muslims. The 1940 Lahore resolution granted Pakistan sovereign state so Muslims could have a separate homeland, and consequently the East Bengali claimed Muslim status to join Pakistan and become free of Hindu competition. But power became concentrated in West Pakistan, and the Bengali had little or no share in education and other social-economic spheres. In spite of the Bengali constituting 54% of the population, Urdu was the only national language of Pakistan, and this time the language controversy was the beginning of the separatist movement. Muslims in East Bengal joined with Hindus in separatist demands based on Bengali linguistic identity, and Bangladesh achieved independence in 1971 as a linguistic unity. To date, no one has raised the point of a united Bengal, because, Kabir points out, neither group (Hindu and Muslim) perceives reunification to be in their best interest. Indeed, almost all group language behavior can be explained on the assumption that people act in their own best and vested interest. This assumption does not always apply to religious groups, at least not in any obvious way. The Hassidim and the Amish both reject mainstream definition of "best interest" as socioeconomic advantage and limit access to education in English (although in different ways) as one means of instead focusing on "best interest" as inner salvation.

We see then an example of a group, East Bengal Muslims, who when they perceived such action best suited to their purposes and demands, claimed religious status and identity and Pakistani nationalism, later linguistic-ethnic nationalism and separatism and, at present, status for Bangladesh founded on religio-linguistic identity.

Other ethno-linguistic groups are not very different from the Bengalis. When they see learning the national language well and fluently in the best interest of their children (and there are social institutions available like the schools and religious organizations, which can help them do so), there are very few problems associated with the educational policies for minority groups, and they become bilingual or shift to the national language.

But when these same groups instead of socioeconomic opportunity see stigmatization, economic exploitation and systematic unemployment, they are perfectly likely to use the original mother tongue as a strategy for mobilization, and language maintenance and language strife become a corollary factor. Language boundary maintenance reinforced with religion is an even stronger tool. The Turks in Europe have frequently followed this latter process (Sachs, 1983).

They practice strict endogamy, often with arranged marriage partners from Turkey, with Islam as the rationale for this endogamy. As we have seen with the Greek Orthodox, such practices serve toward maintaining the minority language or towards slowing the rate of shift.

Almost thirty years ago, Glazer asked: "Just why America produced *without* laws that which other countries, desiring a culturally unified population, were not able to produce *with* laws — is not an easy question" (1966:360). There is a fable by Aesop which holds the answer to that question and which best illustrates the points I have been trying to make. The sun and the wind see a man with a cloak (read language) walking along the road. They decide to enter a contest to see who can first cause him to shed his coat. The wind tears at him for hours but the man only wraps himself more tightly in his cloak. The sun takes over and spreads her benevolence over the man who after a short time divests himself of his cloak. Moral: In hard times, man will cling to his language and ethnic group; in times of plenty, man pays little attention to resources like ethnic languages.

Chapter 3

Ethnicity and Nationalism

Introduction

The past discussion has dealt exclusively with the course of language and the linguistic consequences of ethnic minority groups in prolonged contact within one nation-state. But groups can find another focus of social mobilization than ethnicity, and I here shall argue that there are four distinct types of social mobilization, which under certain specified social conditions result in different linguistic consequences: ethnicity, ethnic movements, ethnic nationalism and geographic nationalism. I am attempting a theoretical framework which will allow us to explain and to predict the language behavior of groups who have access to or are exposed to more than one language. I have argued earlier that such an understanding is vital to helpful educational policies and successful language planning in general.

I have long thought about the social mobilization of religious groups within this framework and eventually opted for considering religion as a social resource similar to language. Linguistic groups may choose a religious identity as the main base in strategies of competition, but they do so as pre-existing ethnic or national groups. *For purposes of explaining language behavior of groups*, I doubt that religion needs to be considered a primary force of group cohesion. More data will help support, modify or disprove this point. Religious groups are also theoretically problematic because of the preponderance of "irrational" behavior where it is difficult to predict behavior on the notion of " acting in their own best interest."

A definite weakness of the framework is the present inability to incorporate the social organization of tribes and clans when those tribes exist within a single ethno-linguistic group spread over several states, such as Kurdistan. Somalia has a clan social organization but with one language within one nation, and so adherents for the various alphabets simply took on aspects of special interest groups which is not theoretically problematic (Laitner, 1977). Nigeria's tribes are isomorphic with ethnic groups and can be so understood. It may be that Kurdish behavior is more explainable with a better understanding of facilitating or constraining social conditions. More data and more reflection are needed on the linguistic consequences of this fairly unusual social organization.

Another weakness is the lack of consideration given to the role of pan-movements in language maintenance. The role of English and French in pan-Africanism, the role of classical and literary standard Arabic in pan-Arabism, and the role of the Chinese character writing system all share certain features, one of which is maintenance beyond what might reasonably have been expected. Future development of the topic of this chapter will have to consider both tribes and pan-movements within the same framework.

Earlier explanations

The focus of social science research and its scholarly writing as it relates to the language behavior of social groups has very much reflected actual events in the real world. The one-nation-one-language national movements of 19th-century Europe provided the beginning of this field of literature, where *nationality* often was used synonymously with *ethnic group* (Deutsch, 1953), as it still tends to be in Russian scholarship.

Fishman has argued for a distinction between *nationalism* and *nationism* in his "Nationality-Nationalism and Nation-Nationism"

(1968), where he attempts to sort out some of the terminological confusion accompanying *nationalism*. He suggests that "the transformation ... of tradition-bound ethnicity to unifying and ideologized nationality ... be called nationalism" (1968:41) and that "wherever politico-geographic momentum and consolidation are in advance of sociocultural momentum and consolidation [be called] *nationism*" (1968:42). He goes on to discuss the different kinds of language problems such recent nation-states face. Van den Berghe in the same volume (1968) also addresses the terminological confusion. He suggests

> that tribe[6] and its derivatives be scrapped altogether. To refer to a political movement based on ethnicity, I shall use the term 'nationalism' (e.g. Yoruba nationalism). To refer to political movements that use the multinational state as their defining unit, I shall speak of 'territorialism' (e.g. Nigerian territorialism)" (1968:215).

Fishman's and van den Berghe's linking of ethnicity with nationalism is typical of the thinking reflected in this set of scholarship.

The concern for nationalism was followed by an interest in ethnicity. Glazer and Moynihan point out in the "Introduction" to their *Ethnicity: Theory and Experience* that the word *ethnicity* made its appearance in the *Oxford English Dictionary* first in the 1972 *Supplement*, where the first recorded usage is of David Riesman in 1953. They suggest "that a new word reflects a new reality and a new usage reflects a change in that reality."

They continue:

> The new word is "ethnicity" and the new usage is the steady expansion of the term "ethnic group" from minority and marginal subgroups at the edges of society — groups expected to assimilate, to disappear, to continue as survivals, exotic or troublesome — to major elements of a society (1975:5).

This concern and focus of research on ethnicity and ethnic minority groups is not only an English language world phenomenon, although the term *ethnicity* may not have been used. To mention just a few representative publications, *Recherches Sociologiques* of Louvain-la-Neuve published in 1977 a special issue on "Langue et Identité Nationale", which deals with language maintenance of ethnic minority groups in Europe. So did the second International Conference on Minority Languages in Åbo/Turko, Finland in 1983 (Molde & Sharp, 1984). *Lenguas y Educación en el Ambito del Estado Español* (Siguan, 1983) deals with the emergent concern for the educational problems of linguistic minority groups in post-Franco Spain. UNESCO in 1984 published a special issue of *Prospects* on "Mother Tongue and Educational Attainment" (14:1, 1984). The Noordwijkerhout Conferences have continued this interest in maintenance and loss of minority languages (Fase, Jaspaert, and Kroon, 1992).

This resurgence of ethnic awareness brings into question the goal of complete assimilation for these groups. Elazar and Friedman discuss this new development of ethnic affirmation (in groups who have all shifted to English) in their *Moving Up: Ethnic Succession in America* (1976). They point out that ethnic identity has often been seen as a problem that must somehow be overcome. Social scientists have often considered religious and ethnic groups as "vestiges of a primitive past that are destined to disappear," (1976:4) but "writers on the 'new pluralism' have argued that racial, religious, and ethnic groups *are* a basic component or our social structure" (p. 5) who affect our institutions and are at times more powerful than economic forces in their influence.

What Elazar and Friedman are discussing in their study of ethnic groups reflects not only a "change in reality", in Glazer and Moynihan's term, but also a paradigm shift (Kuhn, 1970) from equilibrium theory to a conflict perspective. This shift in focus on ethnicity is provocatively explored in John Bennett's *The New Ethnicity: Perspectives from Ethnology* (1975b), whose shift in basic theoretical outlook also reflects the change in the phenomenon of ethnicity. The old notion of ethnicity looked on ethnicity as a group-cultural phenomenon; it was taken to refer to shared norms, artifacts, values, and beliefs within a "culture-population-group frame of reference" (Bennett, 1975a:4), to groups mobilizing around cultural symbols (R. G. Paulston, 1977:181), of which language when it was available formed one of the most obvious. The major function of the new ethnicity can be seen as "a set of strategies for acquiring the resources one needs to survive and to consume at the desired level" (Bennett, 1975a:4); above all, it differs from the old ethnicity in that it is "a cognitive ethnicity, a self-chosen ethnicity" (Bennett, 1975a:9).

And that is roughly where we stand today with the scholarship on the background situation to language problems and educational policies of linguistic subordinate minority groups.[7]

A New Theoretical Framework

I suggest now that there is merit in reconsidering the literature and that instead of entwining the concepts of ethnicity and nationalism, we would be better served in our endeavors to understand the nature of educational policies, if we were to differentiate the two. I suggest four types of social mobilization, which come close to forming a continuum rather than four distinct types:

1. ethnicity which very much corresponds to the notion of old ethnicity;
2. ethnic movement which is based on the concept of the new ethnicity;
3. ethnic nationalism;
4. geographic nationalism which correspond to Kohn's closed and open nationalism (1968) as well as to Fishman's nationalism and nationism (1968; see the chart on page 110).

It is perfectly possible for social groups to embrace a different type of mobilization at different stages of their history and to move back and forth on the continuum of types. No sense of evolution or development is implied in the notion of stage, only time in the historical sense, nor is any ameliorative value implied by any type; ethnicity and nationalism are simply descriptive labels for sets or syndromes of behavior, attitudes and perceptions of groups of peoples. Given certain social conditions, they will behave in certain predictable fashions in regard to language, which behavior it is my purpose to explore.

It is, however, an unavoidable fact that nationalism as a social phenomenon is a stigmatized behavior in present day Western Europe for reasons of historical events during the last century. It is understandable that a region that has experienced the excesses of National Socialism and found economic recovery in a united Europe hesitates to again encourage nationalism. To use nationalism as a concept analytically for organizing sets of behaviors is, however, very different from advocating nationalism as a political and economic system, but it should be recognized that the concept of nationalism may be difficult to use in the present day European climate. I do not intend these comments as a criticism of the analytical power of nationalism, only as a recognition of possible tactical drawbacks when explaining educational policies.

Ethnicity

> An "ethnic group" is a reference group invoked by people who share a common historical style (which may be only assumed), based on overt features and values, and who, through the process of interaction with others, identify themselves as sharing that style. "Ethnic identity" is the sum total of feelings on the part of group members about those values, symbols, and common histories that identify them as a distinct group. "Ethnicity" is simply ethnic-based action (Royce, 1982:18).

Ethnicity tends to stress roots and a shared biological past and the common ancestors (factual or fictional). The basis of personal identity is cultural (including religion), and ethnicity is a matter of self-ascription. The cultural values and beliefs, which are held in common, are unconsciously learned behavior, and ethnicity is just taken for granted. The members tend to feel comfortable with past and future, and there is no opposition and no violence involved.

There is in fact little power struggle and not much purpose with ethnicity, and so the common course is assimilation and concomitant language shift, like the Walloons, who were brought to Sweden in the 1600s to develop the iron industry, have completely assimilated into Swedish culture (Douhan, 1982). Ethnicity will not maintain a language in a multilingual setting if the dominant group allows assimilation, and incentive and opportunity of access to the second language (L2) are present. Some general factors of social conditions which influence access to the L2 were discussed earlier.

Language maintenance and shift in regions where political and socio-economic power is divided between the ethnic groups is difficult and probably impossible to predict. Exogamy, showing definite trends of direction, is the most positive indicator of incipient shift. Once it is clear, for instance, whom the children of migrant workers in Europe will marry, the setting of educational policy will be much facilitated. If they commonly marry nationals of the host culture, there will be no need of special or different educational policies for their children. If, however, they marry exclusively within their own ethnic group, learn the national language poorly and show other trends of strong culture maintenance (arranged marriages with partners from the home country, vacations in the home country, etc.), then a strong case can be argued for the case of bilingual education.[8]

Ethnic Movement

The major difference between ethnicity and ethnic movement is when ethnicity as an unconscious source of identity turns into a conscious strategy, usually in competition for scarce resources. An ethnic movement is ethnicity turned militant, consisting of ethnic discontents who perceive the world as against them, and adversity drawn along ethnic boundaries. While ethnicity stresses the content of the culture, ethnic movements will be concerned with boundary maintenance, in Barth's terms, with "us" against "them". It is very much a conscious, cognitive ethnicity in a power-struggle with the dominant group for social and economic advantage, a struggle which frequently leads to violence and social upheaval. Many ethnic movements have charismatic leaders (probably always born a member of the ethnic group), like Stephen Biko in South Africa and Martin Luther King, but they need not have an intellectual elite or a significant middle class.

Movements need rallying points, and language is a good obvious symbol if it is available. (It may not be. The IRA, the Irish Republican Army, uses English.) So is religion. Original mother tongues and sacred languages are powerful symbols and may serve to support men in their struggle for what they perceive as a better life.[9] But note that language as a symbol need not be the ethnic group's original mother tongue. Both Stephen Biko and Martin Luther King used English and partially for the same reason — the diversity of African languages. The symbol in Biko's case was the choice of language, English rather that Afrikaans; in King's case the symbol lay with the characteristic style of Black English rhetoric, many of which features originated with the West African languages.

When an ethnic movement draws on religion as resource for identity base as a strategy in social competition, when cognitive ethnicity is joined with religious fervor, the likely consequence is one of language maintenance, probably of a sacred language (only).

Sacred languages tend with great diligence to be kept unchanged.[10] The result is that sacred languages often are not spoken and only exist in written form. Groups maintaining a sacred language like the Assyrians will typically shift their everyday language to that of the surrounding community, so that we find Assyrians all maintaining Suryoyo (classical Syrian, closely related to Aramaic) but speaking Arabic, Turkish, Swedish or American English. Maintaining two extra languages seems too cumbersome a task.

There are exceptions. Pre-Israeli Jews maintained both Hebrew and Yiddish (or Hebrew and Ladino) but as a result of externally imposed boundary maintenance, of the environing community's refusal to let them assimilate. (Ladino was after all the result of an earlier assimilation into Spanish culture). When allowed to assimilate, Yiddish disappeared and that explains why Yiddish was maintained in Slavic East Europe but not in Germany, i.e. as a factor of degree of social enclosure (Schermerhorn, 1970). The drop out rate is to likely to be high for such religious groups if the host community allows assimilation, as it is for the Amish and as Bennett (1975b) cites for the New York Hassidim.

Nationalism

When ethnic discontents turn separatist, we get ethnic nationalism. For nationalism, there seems to be as many definitions as there are scholars of nationalism, basically because, in Shafer's words (1972), nationalism has many faces. The following definitions will give a sense of the range of phenomena scholars have attempted to identify:

> [Nationalism is] a consciousness, on the part of individuals or groups, of membership in a nation, or of a desire to forward the strength, liberty, or prosperity of a nation (Royal Institute of International Affairs, 1939).

Arab nationalism emphasized other facets:

> The nation ... is a wider conception than the state, greater than the people, and more meaningful than the fatherland. It is not necessary for a nation to have one state or one fatherland [this is peculiarly Muslim], or to be composed of one people, but it must have its own language [some do not], its own history, its own ideals, its own shared aspirations, its own shared memories, and its own natural links which bind its members in two respects, the moral and the economic (Abd al-Latif Sharara, 1962:228).

African nationalism yet again differs:

> African nationalism is a feeling among the African people. It is not only a feeling against something, but also for something. It is a feeling against European rule ... This is the fundamental feeling of African nationalism — the African feeling against Eurocracy, in favor of Afrocracy ... African nationalism is therefore essentially a political feeling (Sithole, 1960).

Shafer, who has brought together these definitions (1976), concludes elsewhere that it is impossible to fit nationalism into a short definition (1972:5). Kohn points out that while all instances of nationalism will vary according to past history and culture, present social structure and geographical location, all forms of nationalism still share certain traits (1968:64). Cottam's insistence that nationalism not be dealt with as a thing reified but rather interpreted as a manifestation of nationalistic behavior is very useful here as he identifies some of the shared traits in his definition of nationalist "as an individual who sees himself as a member of a political community, a nation, that is entitled to independent statehood, and is willing to grant that community a primary and terminal loyalty" (Cottam, 1964:3). Group cohesion to the end, a goal-orientation of self-determination, a perceived threat of opposing forces, and above all access to or hope of territory are characteristics of all national movements. What is important to remember and what both Royce's and Cottam's definitions stress is that ethnicity and nationalism both are sets or syndromes of behavior, perceptions, and attitudes of a group of people. Given certain social conditions, they will behave in certain predictable fashions, including language behavior which is our present interest.

Both ethnic and geographic nationalism share all these features. The goal is independence, their own political status and social institutions on their own territory. The most common ideal is the nation-state, but there are others. Catalunya, Quebec, and Flemish Belgium are content to remain part of a larger state as long as they can safeguard their own social and cultural institutions of which language (and language maintenance) becomes a very prominent symbol. When use of their own language is denied, other cultural acts acquire a national symbolism way beyond their actual significance. To illustrate, during Franco anti-Catalan days, to cheer for Club Barcelona when the soccer team played Real Madrid became a political statement as was dancing the sardana after Sunday mass.

The improvement of one's own lot in life or at least of one's children's is probably a common goal of all national movements; the motivation, like in ethnic movements, is one of perceived self-interest, a self-chosen state. Very often nationalism takes place as a protest against oppression, against a common enemy, whether it be against a (dominant) group within the same state or against another state. Euskadi, the Basque nation within Spain, is an example of the first type and it introduces another problem of interpretation, the unanimity of degree of intensity of a national movement. The Basques range from terrorists and separatists to assimilists with language shift more common than admitted. There is typically a great emphasis on loyalty and group cohesion, which are consciously taught behaviors, taught through social institutions like school, church, and army, with typical symbols the flag,[11] the national anthem, and above all the language. To admit to language shift is to be disloyal, and this very deep-seated feeling of disloyalty is an additional problem in eliciting valid survey data in this type of research (Thompson, 1974).

Goals in national movements, besides general independence, tend to be quite definite and specific. These goals are often legitimized by or based on historical past events or conditions. During the Finnish school strike in Stockholm during February of 1984, when Finnish parents kept their children out of school in support of their demand for Finnish medium schooling in kindergarten through university level courses, the reason given was that Finland is bilingual in Swedish-Finnish and that Sweden should reciprocate. It is a demand legitimized on the national law of the ethnic immigrant group and its past history and is much more characteristic of nationalism than of ethnic movements, which tend to base their claims on a rationale of equity with others within the nation-state.

Whether a defining characteristic or a necessary social condition, a national movement must have a well-developed middle class in which condition it differs from ethnic movements. Alba's (1975) anecdote of the Catalan workers who considered issues of language immaterial is representative. "We don't care if we are exploited in Castilian or Catalan," was their rejoinder, and they aligned themselves with the workers' unions and the socialist party rather than mobilize themselves along national lines. Without a stake in property, nationalism is not perceived to further one's self-interest.

Royce considers the similar situation of the Basques. The ETA, the Basque national organization is led by members of the middle class. The lower class perceived no advantage in a Basque movement, and the concerns and economic interests of the elite are primarily state/national and international. The regional economic interests are in the control of the middle class who feel that they carry an unfair share of Spain's economic burden with no adequate compensation. "The important point in this case is that the impetus for ethnic nationalism came from the sector whose privileges and power depended on the economic well-being of the Basque provinces. Basque nationalism was the obvious way to maintain their position" (Royce, 1982:104).

The crucial difference between ethnic movement and ethnic nationalism is access to territory; without land one cannot talk about Basque nationalism. It is also access to territory that gives viability to a separatist movement. We can talk about Chicano nationalism but without territory such a movement, were it genuine, is doomed to failure. Mostly such phraseology masks conceptual confusion and what is intended is a label for what in fact is an ethnic movement fighting for equal access to goods and services (Oriol, 1979).

Ethnic nationalism and geographic nationalism share a great many features as is obvious from the previous discussion. The difference between them is probably the same as Hans Kohn outlines for "open" and "closed" nationalism (1968:66). In ethnic or closed nationalism the ethnic group is isomorphic with the nation-state. The emphasis is on the nation's autochthonous character, on the common origin and ancestral roots. In ethnic nationalism language can come to carry an importance way beyond any proportion of its communicative functions. The typical claim is that the deep thoughts and the soul of the nation can only be adequately expressed in the common mother tongue. Hitler's Germany was the most extreme form of ethnic nationalism with its emphasis on racial exclusivism and rootedness in the ancestral soil. (It is an interesting observation that the leaders of national movements need not be original members of that nation; Hitler and Stalin did not have their original roots in the state of which they became national leaders.)

Kohn calls "open" nationalism a more modern form; it is territorially based (hence geographic nationalism) and features a political society, constituting a nation of fellow citizens regardless of ethnic descent. The so-called great immigration countries of Canada, Australia and the Unites States are good examples. As Kohn comments, they rejected the notion of a nation based on a common past, a common religion or a common culture. Instead "[Americans] owe their nationhood to the affirmation of the modern trends of emancipation, assimilation, mobility, and individualism" (1968:66).

In ethnic nationalism, language is a prime symbol of the nation but that is not necessarily so with geographic nationalism. Actually, the United States does not even legally have a national language, although at present two major national organizations, U.S. English and English First, are working to support passage of legislation to make English the official language of the U.S.A. (Crawford, 1992). This official-English debate is causing considerable controversy, where the English-only movements are accused of imposing cultural tyranny and enforced assimilation while they in turn consider the minorities divisive for the country and in the late Senator S.I. Hayakawa's words "sheep in wolfs' clothing"; Hayakawa proposed a constitutional amendment in 1981, designating English as the official language of the U.S.A., an amendment which failed. Presently seventeen states have official English laws in effect with more states scheduled for voting on the issue (Brochetti, 1992; Piatt, 1990). Since in fact the immigrants are more than eager to learn English, the liberal position is that it is a non-problem and argues for English Plus (Cazden & Snow, 1990).

Canada has two national languages, but English and French are not thought of as national symbols of Canada. Rather, the maintenance of a common language was primarily undertaken for pragmatic LWC purposes. At the same time, although one cannot change one's genes, one can learn a new language, and in a nation which does not care about genes but uses language to define its membership, as Catalunya does, learning the new language obviously held both practical and symbolic significance: knowing the national language became the hallmark of membership and in-group membership, and easy access to the new language has tended to result in very rapid bilingualism, often with consequent shift.

Conclusion

M. Pompidou is said to have commented that a politician can ruin himself in three ways, with women, by taking bribes, and by planning. Women, he said, is the most pleasant way, gambling the quickest, and planning the surest. What this anecdote illustrates is the uncertainty inherent in planning at the national level, a fact recognized by any experienced politician at the same time as he faces the necessity for such long-range planning.

I have argued in this chapter that the uncertainty of language planning in education will be reduced if the planners consider the social context of language problems and especially the social, cultural and economic forces which contribute to language maintenance and shift. The most elegant educational policies for minority groups are doomed to failure if they go counter to prevailing social forces, especially the economic situation. This is as true for maintenance efforts in an economically incorporating group as it is for shift efforts to the national language for a socially marginal group. In OECD countries, the language planning efforts most likely to be successful are those which are supported by economic advantage (or similar social incentives) for the minority groups.

At the same time, planners need to acknowledge and respect the fact that there are other points of view on language maintenance and shift than the strictly pragmatic aspects argued in this chapter. Religious groups take language maintenance seriously without any immediately obvious incentives, and so do a few ethnic group. States vary in their actual tolerance of religious disparity, but the principle of religious freedom is well recognized. Simply, it is one of respect for the self-determination of a group to hold the values and beliefs as it chooses. Similarly, we should hold the truth self-evident that an ethnic group has a right to its own language if it so chooses. The point made here that ethnic groups very rarely opt for continued language maintenance if the social conditions favor a shift to the national language is no counter-argument to the ethical principle of a right for minority groups to cultural self-determination. However, planners need to realize that the social costs of such continued language and culture maintenance tend to be high to the minority group members, and consequently parents and children may be at variance on this point, a situation which enormously complicates the setting of educational policy.

While moral decency dictates the language rights of minority groups, it does not necessarily follow that the state is under any obligation to economically support such rights, nor does it follow that minority groups have a right to impose their language on the nation. The context of the situation and its historical development will hold the key to such problems, which are invariably political in nature rather than linguistic. Honest planning does not confuse the two.

PART II

Introduction

> Thus, by judiciously contrasting groups, sociocultural processes and types of contact situations (not necessarily taken two at a time, if higher level interaction designs prove to be feasible) it should become possible to more meaningfully apportion the variance in language maintenance or language shift outcomes. Furthermore, the greater our insight with respect to socio-cultural processes and the more appropriate our typology of intergroup contact situations, the more possible it becomes to meaningfully assemble and analyze language maintenance and language shift files. Such files would permit both cross-cultural and diachronic analysis, of primary as well as of secondary data, based upon comparable data, collected and organized in accord with uniform sets of socio-cultural processes and contact categories. This state of affairs is still far off but it is the goal toward which we might attempt to move...
>
> (Fishman, 1971:330)

Part II intends to contrast and compare a number of case studies for clarification of their diverse courses of mother tongue maintenance. It particularly seeks to illustrate the type of social mobilization discussed in chapter 3 and touches on the classic question of sociology which is so frequently ignored in sociolinguistics, "under what social conditions?"

In the study of language maintenance and shift, we either know what the trends or results are in individual cases, or we know how to find out, but we have a poor understanding of the causal factors. Basically, the problem is the search for independent variable(s) which can be generalized to other situational contexts. Urbanization, for instance, is a commonly suggested causal factor in bringing about language shift (although I see it as intervening). However, there is not always agreement whether formal aspects of the language itself in question is an independent or dependent variable and whether social factors and behavior constitute cause or effect. Most ignored of all are the intervening or contextual variables,[12] the answer to "under what social conditions?", which we are beginning to see profoundly influence the linguistic outcomes of ethnic groups in contact.

Grimshaw discusses some of the basic perspectives on the causal relationship between structure and language:

> (1) that which sees language as fundamental (or as a source, cause, independent variable [or set of independent variables]...(2) that which sees social structure as determinant or as independent variable [or set of independent variables], (3) that which sees neither as prior to the other, both being seen as co-occurring and co-determining.... (1971:95)

It is possible to add a fourth perspective, as Grimshaw does, which sees the first and second perspective in a chain of interactions where social structure or behavior affects language which in turn affects social behavior. An example can be found in the present status of English as a world language. The social factors after World War II of British and American military power, economic status, and ex-colonial influence contributed to the development of English as the world's major lingua franca. Today, the status of English as a world language (quite divorced from the social status of Britain and the United States) has contributed to millions of school children learning English as a foreign language for pragmatic reasons.

A similar perspective is probably the most accurate to account for all phenomena in the process of language maintenance and language shift. For instance, structural power will lead to selection, standardization, and literature of a language which in turn will bestow literary prestige and language loyalty on a language which in turn will contribute to language maintenance or slower rate of shift. However, until our theories are more comprehensive and our understanding clearer about the causal factors in language shift, such a linked perspective may easily contribute to confusion rather than clarification. In these chapters, I will consider social structure, specifically the types of social

Introduction

group mobilization, as the determinant variables and the differential linguistics outcomes as the resultant or dependent variables. In assessing the theoretical framework which spells out this relationship, I wish to examine, i.e. to contrast and compare, these case studies in order to account for their differential linguistic outcomes.

The comparison of case studies is probably the major approach to the study of language maintenance and shift at any theoretical level. "Although the study of language maintenance or language shift *need* not be completely limited to the comparison of separate cases it is nevertheless undeniably true that the comparative method is quite central to inquiry within this topic area" (Fishman, 1971:327). The case studies themselves usually document maintenance or shift of individual situations and usually attempt to identify some causal factors, but we recognize that such findings may hold limited generalizability unless they are tested against some higher level theoretical explanation. Besides the search for causal factors, another major task is to identify and eventually typologize under what social conditions maintenance or shift takes place. This approach necessitates an analysis of case studies in light of some guiding hypotheses.

The guiding hypotheses I propose were discussed in chapter 3 for explaining and predicting the language behavior of ethnic groups in contact within a contemporary (nation)state; namely that linguistic groups can form four distinct types of social mobilization: ethnicity, ethnic movements, ethnic nationalism and geographic nationalism; which under certain specified social conditions result in differential linguistic outcomes of language maintenance or shift.

The key test cases are in the chapter comparing Catalan and Occitan. As I discuss in the Preface, it was my initial failure to account for the unusual language maintenance of Catalan in terms of ethnic boundary maintenance which eventually led to the writing of this book. I had originally chosen to work on Catalan for trivial reasons: I had sabbatical leave, wanted a place where both my husband and I could do fieldwork, where the children had access to schools, etc. So I found myself after six months' fieldwork with a case study but no explanation.

Working out that explanation, i.e. the model building of chapter 3, took close to ten years till I was satisfied. The rest of the test cases were chosen because I had field experience (except Ireland), because in some cases I had already been asked to do some work, but most of all because they just plain interested me. It should be clear though, that if the theoretical framework is solid enough, any case studies of language maintenance and shift in a multilingual country should serve to illustrate the same principles.

Tanzania is an unusual case for Africa with an indigenous language as the successful national language. It illustrates as well the importance of not having vested interest groups, i.e. tribal, in the development of nationalism and successful language policy.

Peru is very much a country of ethnicity without economic rewards and shift to Spanish. The Amerindian situation there is representative of most of the Americas.

Sweden — except for the Finns — is basically the same phenomenon as Peru, i.e. ethnicity, but with a very different population, immigrants, and a much more rapid shift.

Finally, Ireland for which there are many claims of the revival of Irish, is another case of shift. Government policies simply are not able to revive Irish.

These four case studies represent four very different situations but the same model serves to explain the success or failure of their language and educational policies.

Chapter 4

Catalan and Occitan

Comparative Test Cases for a Theory of Language Maintenance and Shift

Introduction

I here wish to account for language variance in language maintenance and shift by examining the two cases of Catalan and Occitan in light of the previously discussed analytical framework. The general question concerns the reasons the speakers of some languages tenaciously cling to their ancestral languages (Brudner, 1972), while others slowly (Dorian, 1981) or rapidly (Fishman, 1966; Lieberson and Curry, 1971; Veltman, 1983) abandon them. When shift takes place within groups who do not possess another territorial base, we have a case of language death, which helps explain the emotional nature and lack of objectivity in much of the writing about threatened languages.

The basic proposition deals with the language consequences of linguistic minorities in prolonged contact within one nation-state: subordinate groups for whom the basic focus of social mobilization is ethnicity are likely to shift to the language of the dominant group, given motivation and opportunity, while groups whose social focus is a sense of nationalism are more likely to maintain the ethnic minority language. My claim here is that Catalunya[13] represents a case of nationalism and language maintenance while Occitania is a case of ethnicity (with some ethnic movement) and consequent widespread language shift to French with language death an imminent likelihood.

The analysis is based on some primary but mostly secondary data and on six months' fieldwork in 1978. It was my initial failure to account for Catalan language maintenance in terms of ethnic boundary maintenance that eventually led me to the present problem formulation.

Catalan and Occitan make ideal comparison cases in that the languages are closely related Romance languages, both co-existing with other Romance languages, Spanish and French. In this way, linguistic features can be held steady, as it were, and have the same potential for influence. Comparing Catalan to Basque, for instance, would leave open the possibility that it is for linguistic rather than social reasons so many fewer immigrants learn Basque than learn Catalan, Basque being a non-Indo-European language and much more difficult for a Spanish speaker to learn than Catalan (Shabad and Gunther, 1982). The areas are geographically contiguous and have a partially shared history. Religion, which so often is a confounding factor in language maintenance, is not a variable; Catalan and Occitan speakers share the Roman Catholicism of their nation-states Spain and France. So we can be reasonably assured that the socio-structural differences we turn up may be determinant variables in accounting for language maintenance and shift.

Occitan

> [Les] auteurs expriment la conviction que le monde occitan a en quelque sorte une mission humaine, que ses valeurs constituent un patrimoine mondial et que l'occitanisme aurait tort de se considérer simplement comme la négation du monde français. (Abel, 1973:58)

Occitania is the southern region of France where langue d'oc or Occitan was originally spoken running from the area of Bordeaux and fanning out in several isoglosses to the East to define the area known as Franco-Provençal. Dialect variability has always been considerable and pan-dialectal comprehension has traditionally been an important part of linguistic competence (Eckert, 1983:290). Historically, the language (and the region) had its day of glory during the 12th century when the troubadours led the world in literary brilliance with their poetry. Posner points out that even then the literary language the troubadours used was not the same variety as Provençal proper, the dialect of the Marseille area, and that most of the poetry was written within a fifty-year span (1966:255). The end of Provençal tradition of lyric poetry and courtly love came with the Albigensian Crusade, sanctioned by Pope Innocent III and carried out by northern French armies. The Northern motivation in defeating the South was no doubt political (rather than concerned with religious heresies), and after the defeat at Muret in 1213, the South never again recovered literary and cultural hegemony, although Provençal continued as a spoken language. With the Ordinance of Villers-Cotterets in 1539, which decreed that all legal documents were to be in French, French became de facto the official written language of Occitania. The motivation may have been pragmatic and non-chauvinistic, but the result was "an enormous contribution to the diffusion of French and the linguistic unification of France" (Gordon, 1978:24), as well as great diversification and multiplication of dialects in Occitania where Occitan continued to be spoken. French was standardized by the French Academy under Louis XIV, and after the French Revolution, the National Convention in 1793-94 legislated the teaching of French throughout France. Patois was considered a barrier to social mobility and participatory democracy, and non-French dialects were stigmatized. Writes Gordon: "According to Robert Lafont, 'The historical realization of France is, in effect, a long and methodical destruction of national entities of other races within the territorial hexagon'" (1978:31). But it was national free education, introduced into Occitania in the latter part of the 19th century, which became the primary social institution to provide access to French and the major agent for language shift. The motivation was economic: the primarily agricultural economy could not compete with the industrialized North, and French was necessary for outmigration, for upward social mobility:

> ...Pendant des siècles, la raison d'abandonner leur langue était sociale pour les Occitans, et l'abandon commença d'abord dans la noblesse pour passer à la bourgeoisie, puis aux classes moyennes et finalement aux ouvriers. Maintenant, il n'en est plus de même, a l'exception des régions archaisantes. Ce qui tue la langue, ce sont les moyens modernes de diffusion de la pensée, presse industrialisée, radio, cinéma, télévision qui vont au plus profond des campagnes comme véhicule d'un francais imposé aux consciences; ce sont les pénétrations d'une population permanente de fonctionnnaires déracinés, d'ouvrieres étrangers et maintenant d'entreprises agricoles qui s'installent dans les réserves les plus reculées; ce sont les arrivées périodiques de touristes. On peut penser que la langue, abandonnée a sa simple resistance naturelle, en est à son dernier soupir et que les hommes de notre génération pourront assister a sa mort. La mort de l'occitan est écrite dans le procès entamé depuis des siécles et de plus en plus accélérée depuis vingt ans (Bec, 1967:122-123).

Today, two studies, Schlieben-Lange (1977) and Eckert (1980), have found that most of the younger members of the Occitan speech community are monolingual French speakers: "The adult population of the community is consciously transitional — they have encouraged their children to leave the region to find work, and in preparation for this they have raised them as monolingual French speakers" (Eckert, 1980:1059). Occitan, writes Eckert, was shamed out of existence:

> Linguistic shame was exercised in a series of social opposition associated with the domains of the language: French was the language of the outside, the rich, the educated; Occitan was the language of the home, the poor, the uneducated. (Eckert, 1983:294)

During the past fifteen or twenty years, there has been an Occitan movement to promote the use of the language. As early as 1951, the Loi Deixonne provided for the optional teaching of Occitan, but regionalists complained during the seventies that the implementation of the law was inadequate, as it indeed was, with lack of teacher training, inconvenient class time, etc. (Gordon, 1978:100). Abel writes in 1973 that only those born before 1925 and living in rural villages know how to speak Occitan and that only those belonging to the Occitan movement know how to write Occitan (1973:23). The real problem, from his viewpoint, is the fact that the intellectuals and academics who are the militant occitanists "do not represent the parties of the population for whom Occitan is still the language of daily use" (Abel, 1973:58).

The written standard form of Occitan is so divergent from its spoken dialects that its speakers feel equally alienated from the movement's Occitan as they do from French. French is associated with modernity and opportunity, Occitan with the shame they still remember when the teacher hung a wooden shoe around their neck in punishment for speaking Occitan in school (Eckert, 1980). Their children only know French. Only an incurable optimist would think that the future of Occitan was uncertain; it is facing extinction, unless there is a drastic change in the economy.[14]

Catalan

Catalan, a Romance language closely related to Occitan and to Spanish, is spoken in Catalunya, situated in the north-eastern part of Spain. It is also spoken in Valencia and the Balearic Islands, parts of Sardinia, in the Roussillon area of France and in Andorra, where it is the official language. Valenciano and Mallorqui are occasionally considered separate languages by their speakers and need not concern us here; the official language of Sardinia is Italian and of Roussillon French, where Catalan seems to follow the same course as Occitan (Posner, 1966:259). Peculiarly enough, the language of Andorra is typically ignored in maintenance efforts such as textbook writing and discussions about language in Catalunya; e.g., Siguan in his introduction to "Language and education in Catalonia" (1984) does not mention Andorra in his account of where Catalan is spoken. Dialect differences never have been much of a concern, maybe because the Catalan of the 'great epoch' was remarkable for its uniformity and lack of dialectalization. Whether this came about only because of "the imposition of a 'chancery standard' is difficult to say" (Posner, 1966:259). Certainly dialects did develop during the times when Castilian was the official administrative language, but now Siguan can write about Catalan: "It is fully systematized with its own dictionary, grammar and orthography, which are accepted without dispute..." (1984:108). The number of Catalan speakers varies with the source:

> Given that the national census (Instituto Nacional de Estadistica) does not collect information on linguistic affiliation or cross tabulate data of place of birth and place of residence, the figures for Catalan speakers which are to be found in the literature must be regarded as informed estimates. (Pi-Sunyer, 1971:115)

Pi-Sunyer estimates six million Catalan inhabitants out of a total population in Spain of thirty-three million, McNair (1980) similarly posits a population over five million out of a total of thirty-four million from the 1970 census, while Siguan in 1984 suggests a population of nine million.

Catalunya developed as the Spanish March, a bufferblock between Muslim Spain and France. The County of Barcelona was joined by marriage with Provence (where I have seen the Catalan flag still flown) and later with the kingdom of Aragon in 1137. It became a major Mediterranean mercantile nation during the 13th and 14th centuries, and Middle Catalan flourished during the 13th to 15th century with serious work written in science and philosophy. Catalan was also used for administration and law.

During the late 15th century, with the marriage of Ferdinand of Aragon and Catalunya to Isabella of Castile in 1469, the center of political gravity shifted to Madrid and Castile, and changes took place "which transformed an important Mediterranean state into a dependent principality and finally into a cluster of Spanish provinces" (Pi-Sunyer, 1971:122). "Upper-class Catalans who increasingly came into contact with the Castilian elite over matters of economic affairs came to prefer the use of Spanish" (Taylor, 1984:3).

In 1716, Philip V of the new Bourbon dynasty followed the French model of linguistic unity and issued a decree which forbade the use of Catalan: "Books in Catalan must be forbidden, nor must it be spoken or written in schools and instruction in Christian doctrine must be in Castilian" (Read, 1978:152). Catalan remained politically repressed (with a brief interlude during the Second Spanish Republic 1931-1039) until the death of General Franco in 1975. Nevertheless, with the advent of industrialization in the 18th century, Catalunya eventually became the most prosperous region in Spain. Concomitant with the economic recovery, a cultural and linguistic renaissance, *La Renaixenca*, took place, which merged with *Catalanisme*, "a community awareness...spurred on by the new middle classes" (Siguan, 1984:105). In spite of the political repression of Catalan, which Vallverdú termed persecuted bilingualism during the early Franco regime (1973:140), the Catalans refused to give up their language, and a study in 1979 (Shabad and Gunther, 1982) showed that 97% of native Catalans spoke the language and that 78% of all residents did so regardless of place of birth. Another survey found that from 45%-50% of school children in Catalunya are Catalan speakers. The latter figure reflects the massive migration into Catalonia from the rest of Spain (McNair, 1980:25).

Article 3 of the 1978 Spanish Constitution decrees Castilian and the regional languages to be both official within their community. The Statutes of Autonomy of Catalunya, promulgated in 1979, state:

> The specific language of Catalonia is Catalan.
> The Spanish language is the official language throughout the Spanish state.

> The Generalitat (Autonomous Government) of Catalonia will guarantee the normal and official use of both languages. It will take the necessary measures to ensure knowledge of them and will establish conditions such as will bring about their complete equality with respect to the duties and rights of the citizens of Catalonia. (Siguan, 1984:109)

Clearly, Catalan is doing very well. While there are problems primarily with implementation in the educational sector and with the large number of Castilian speaking immigrants from the rest of Spain, there is no indication other that the continued maintenance of Catalan.

Comparison

Ethnicity or nationalism

Based on my discussion of defining characteristics for ethnicity and nationalism, I propose here to argue that Occitania is a case of ethnicity while Catalunya manifests the characteristics of nationalism, following in general the outline of that discussion.

Both Catalunya and Occitania share the notion of a "Glorious Past" which is very much part of their consciousness. Indeed, Abel can claim:

> ...que l'habitant de la région de Toulouse a en général une certaine notion du fait qu'il vit dans une région qui a son histoire propre. J'irais même jusqu' à supposer que cette région "historique" a plus de réalite pour lui que par exemple la région "administrative" moderne. (1973:14)

One of my favorite bar/restaurants in Barcelona was called *Mare Nostrum* 'Our sea', a common appellation in Catalunya which refers to the time during the Middle Ages when the Mediterranean literally was their sea. Their glorious past is an important part of their present.

They also share territory. But while Catalunya has experienced considerable in-migration from the rest of Spain since the 19th century, Occitania has witnessed massive out-migration during this century. And there the important similarities end.

The Occitans do not emphasize a different cultural personality and they look to Paris and things French for direction and guidance. If anything, they emphasize "a human mission" and universal values which transcend mere regionalism. They do not feel a sense of speech community but rather a sense of "historic region" (Abel, 1973:14). There is little sense of ethnic pride (except historically), and Eckert documents the sense of linguistic shame and the association of Occitan with being poor and uneducated (1983:285). In contrast, the Catalans avoid direction from Madrid and look to Paris and Western Europe for cultural inspiration. They take great pleasure in emphasizing cultural values different from the rest of Spain, to the point of stereotyping:

> Catalans are often characterized by both insiders and outsiders as ambitious, intelligent, sensible, industrious people. Catalans themselves are very proud of what they see as one of their most traditional traits, *seny*. Literally "sense", it refers to level-headed, feet-on-the-ground common sense (Woolard,1986:17).

The work ethic, negotiation and compromise are all time-honored traditions. They are very stubborn and proud of it. Most important, the sense of shame Eckert discusses for Occitan is totally absent for the Catalans: "There are few Catalans who doubt that they are in some way 'better' that Castilians (the hereditary enemy?)" (Pi-Sunyer, 1978:personal communication).

It is in fact an open question how much ethnicity Occitan children feel who are monolingual in French. The historical identity is clear, but whether a sense of ethnicity is surviving language shift is more uncertain. Another question is whether *le mouvement occitaniste*, the Occitan movement, actually merits the term of ethnic movement. It is primarily an intellectual/academic movement (intellectual leaders are not needed for ethnic movements) and it lacks such typical characteristics as an ethnic boundary maintenance, power struggle, militance and violence, and my interpretation is that it is not seen as strategy in competition for scarce resources but rather as a renewal of cultural identity for its own sake. Asks Touraine:

> Since the Occitanist movement is incapable of creating a party or an organized movement, and since it is torn apart by the political and unionist conflicts spreading throughout the French left, and is still as much divided between "political" and "cultural" adherents as it was twenty years ago — and far more than it was ten years ago — can it be said that the movement really exists? (Touraine, 1985:159)

While Occitan is associated with peasants and poor workers (besides the intellectual), Catalan is solidly middle class as well as working class: "Since the features of the Catalan character were most fully codified for the 19th century bourgeoisie, whose family-based mercantile and industrial enterprises marked them off from the wealthy land-owning class of the rest of Spain, it has been difficult to extricate Catalan identity from its bourgeois background" (Woolard, 1986:19). The *Bandera Roja* party (the Catalan communist branch) at one time engaged "in the exclusive use of the Spanish language explaining to all and sundry that Catalan was 'the language of the bourgeoisie', and therefore to be avoided" (Giner, 1980:47). The history of Catalunya is a history of landowning farmers, of artisans, shopkeepers, workshop owners (the *menestralia*), of merchants and industrialists, of a concern for the serious business of making money. Not only does Catalunya exhibit the basic defining characteristics of nationalism as territory, intellectual leaders (exiled during Franco), a middle class and property, stubborn loyalty, a common enemy (which Franco did his best to justify), a cultural "external distinction, internal cohesion" (Haugen, 1966),[15] and a goal-orientation of political self-determination, she perceives of herself as a nation. Woolard, in her work on language and ethnicity in Catalunya, writes in a footnote:

> It is difficult to eliminate confusion over terminology in discussing Catalonia, "Nation" and "Nationalism" in this chapter always refer to Catalonia and to Catalanist political sentiment, not to Spain or Spanish-oriented loyalty. "Nationalism" has been used rather than "regionalism" because Catalan political activists conceive of their homeland as a nation. While the term is rarely defined, it is often invoked in debate and is a tremendously powerful concept for both supporters and opponents of Catalan nationhood (Woolard, 1986:34)

Since Catalunya's history and development includes a variety of ethnic groups (Romans, Visigoths, Occitans, French, Castilians, Italians, Jews), this sense of nationalism is not ethnically but territorially based, similar to the U.S., in fact. Writing about "open" nationalism, Kohn's comments about the Americans equally well apply to the Catalans: "[They] owe their nationhood to the affirmation of the modern trends of emancipation, assimilation, mobility, and individualism" (1968:66). It is only that the Catalans were modern very early on; Giner (1980) makes the case that they were the first capitalists in Europe, and one can argue the case that Catalan nationalism was well in effect before the industrial revolution. In geographic nationalism, speaking the national language (whether official or not) is an important marker of group membership, and in the past immigrants to Catalunya have typically learned Catalan in addition to Castilian. At present, under the Statutes of Autonomy of Catalonia, 1979, there is increased social and political pressure for the use of Catalan:

> Social class enters into these language policy considerations in another way as well; in both the public and private sector of the Catalan economy, access to white-collar jobs is being increasingly restricted to those reasonably fluent in Catalan.....a disproportionately large number of non-Catalan-speaking immigrants have low-status occupations (Shabad and Gunter, 1982:468,470).

The basic incentive for learning Catalan for the immigrants is economic, just as it was for learning French for the Occitan speakers. In Brudner's terms: Jobs select language learning strategies (1972). But it is far from clear that economic incentives are sufficient for language maintenance, and although it is rare that superordinate groups in a favored economic position do shift languages, it happens as with the Normans in England. Rather, economic incentives are probably a necessary but not sufficient condition for language maintenance, and my argument is that the set of behavior, attitudes and perceptions which we associate with nationalism provides that sufficient condition. In the words of Pi-Sunyer:

> The lesson from Catalonia is not that economic and political forces should be disregarded—on the contrary, they should be studied with consummate care—but that these alone will not explain the phenomenon of nationalism. Not because nationalism does not respond to these forces, but because they will be interpreted and altered by specific cultures and societies-which are themselves undergoing change (Pi-Sunyer, 1985:273).

In this chapter I have argued that as a result of geographic nationalism Catalan has been maintained as a viable language of Catalunya in spite of centuries of political repression. Its history, social structure, economy and possibly cultural stubbornness have been contributing factors.

Occitan, on the other hand, is dying and in the absence of any national movement, a weak ethnicity and mainly historical sense of identity are not sufficient to halt the shift to French where lie all the economic rewards.

Chapter 5

Case Studies

Tanzania, Peru and Sweden

I earlier discussed language and religion as social resources, using the example of nationalistic movements in Bangladesh and made the point that other ethnic groups are not very different from the Bengalis. When they see learning the national language well and fluently in the best interest of their children, there are very few problems associated with the educational policies for minority groups. Within the single city-state of Singapore with her four official languages and three major religions, there is no sign of ethnic strife or educational problems (Crewe, 1977). In fact, the ex-colonial English is favored as medium of instruction. I must admit that I looked very carefully for competition along ethnic lines but saw none. The simple explanation is to be found in Singapore's very strong and expanding economy. There is enough of the good of this life to go around for everybody, and competition takes place on the basis of individual qualities, not along ethnic lines.

But when these same ethnic groups instead of socioeconomic opportunity perceive social discrimination, economic exploitation and systematic unemployment, they are perfectly likely to use the original mother tongue as a strategy for mobilization. It is not that mainstream members and those from assimilated former ethnic groups like the Poles and the Slovaks in Pittsburgh do not face difficulties in a declining economy; it is rather that they do not feel injustice and antagonism, and also that they have (through language shift) lost language as a resource for mobilization strategy. A while ago, City Council decided to merge the Police Force and the Fire Fighter units in Pittsburgh. Both groups perceived this as being against their best interests and violently opposed the new policy. As both groups share the same ethnic mix, language and ethnicity were not available resources and instead both groups mobilized along the lines of their labor unions. Had ethnicity been an available resource, they very likely would have mobilized along ethnic lines, to judge from Elazar and Friedman's (1976) case study of teachers in Philadelphia who did just that and who were able to successfully defend their jobs in that fashion.

The basic point to be made is that ethnic groups use language when available as a social resource when it is to their perceived advantage to do so, not otherwise. I would like here to examine some case studies to illustrate this point and others that follow from it.

Tanzania

> In opting for Swahili as its sole official and national language, Tanzania has most departed from policies established under colonial rule. Although English is still the medium of post-primary education (and its role was re-affirmed in 1983), its overall position has been reduced. This also applies to the vernaculars. The uniform practice of using Swahili is a symbol of both socioeconomic egalitarianism and national integration, reflecting the nation's socialistic policies. (Scotton, 1988:219)

Tanzania represents a case of successful choice and implementation of a national and official indigenous language in Africa and as such is a rare case, since most sub-Sahara African states have an ex-colonial language as national language. Some reasons for the ex-colonial language choice are: (1) vested interest of elite groups, (2) textbooks and curricula already in place, (3) the economic costs of standardizing languages(s), printing textbooks and training teachers, (4) language attitudes of prestige of the colonial languages and their use as international languages, and (5) finally, and in many cases most importantly, their use as trans-ethnic languages (Bokamba, 1981; Scotton, 1988).

Swahili is a Bantu language, used as a lingua franca for about 25 million ethnically diverse people living in East Africa (besides Tanzania, Swahili is a national language in Kenya and also spoken in Uganda, Burundi, Ruanda, Zambia, Somalia, Mozambique and Zaire) (Hinnebusch, 1979; Whiteley, 1969). It is a native language for some 2 million people on Zanzibar and on the East African coast from Somalia to Mozambique, with many dialects, which was part of the problems of later standardization. Swahili as a lingua franca predates the rise of modern education and independent national government. It developed as a trade language in the monsoon trade, controlled by Arabs, with Arabia, India, Malaysia, China and Indonesia. The ruling class was mixed Arab-African, and Swahili language and culture spread as trade and town spread, and a new civilization evolved, ethnically diverse, maritime, Muslim, urban, mercantile, literate in Arabic with a writing tradition for Swahili in Arabic script. (Later, the European missionaries in control of education during early colonization changed that.) Zanzibar came to dominate trade and inland trade and sent large trading caravans (Sw. *safari*) inland as far as Zaire and Zambia for ivory and slaves. They used the Zanzibar dialect of Swahili.

When the missionaries arrived in the 1860s, they needed a language for communication, and they settled on Swahili as the most practical choice. By the 1890s, the Germans had administrative control of then Tanganyika, and the German administrators and settlers along with the missionaries were learning Swahili. Swahili newspapers were founded, and village headmen made reports in Swahili. Schools used Swahili as medium of instruction. The colonial administration (first the German and consequently the English) followed this practice and used Swahili to reach the people (Abdulaziz, 1971; O'Barr, 1976; Polome & Hill, 1980). (This was not so in Kenya and Uganda where English was used.) Under the German administration, Swahili was sufficient for membership in the junior civil service, while beyond that level a knowledge of German was needed. The British required both Swahili and English for junior civil service. Consequently, an attitude developed that Swahili was second best, but in Tanzania where the Germans had used Swahili as medium of instruction, there was a positive attitude toward the language as academically capable.

In 1961, Tanganyika became a republic with J. Nyerere as president, in 1964 Tanganyika and Zanzibar became the United Republic of Tanzania, and in 1977, President Nyerere's socialist Chama Cha Mapinduzi Party (CCM) was granted political supremacy by the constitution. The official language planners in Dar es Salaam explained to me as socialist philosophy the rationale for the use of Swahili "the need to consolidate the base, i.e. general literacy for the masses" (presumably a requirement for socialism and equity), but they also pragmatically saw the need "to maintain the elite infrastructure (i.e. in English) for the study of engineering, veterinary medicine, agriculture, and medicine" (Fieldnotes, Dar es Salaam, 1986). If anything, I saw a concern that they had been too successful with Swahili, and that efforts now were directed towards English.

The language planning success with Swahili in Tanzania contrasts with the failure in neighboring Kenya, which failure is probably due to two main reasons: (1) ethnic strife along tribal boundaries, i.e. vested interest groups, which use language as a resource for competition; and (2) language attitudes as a result of colonial policy, which accord English all prestige and see Swahili as a way of keeping African-American in their place (Whiteley, 1974).

One can of course interpret the success in Tanzania as a result of socialist philosophy, but it would be inaccurate as the success predates the CCM. Rather it was a historical accident of the coming together of a number of factors: (1) There was an indigenous language available with a centuries' long tradition as a lingua franca; (2) the language was already standardized and had been used as a medium of education by the missionaries and the Germans with concomitant positive attitudes; (3) Swahili is a Bantu language of the same language family as most of the 130-plus languages spoken in Tanzania and therefore easy to learn (The Kenyans make much of how hard it is to learn Swahili for non-Bantu speakers, but it should be mentioned as an aside that the Maasai in Tanzania seem to have no difficulty); (4) although the British supplanted Swahili with English, it was still, or maybe because of it, relatively easy for Nyerere and his socialist movement for independence to embrace Swahili as a symbol of nationalism and freedom from oppression; (5) maybe most importantly, Swahili was not the native language of any one dominant group (only 12,000 speakers on the mainland), and among the 130 tribes, there is really no clearly dominant group so they escape the curse of special interest groups; (6) finally, there is in the urban centers considerable intermarriage between tribal members, and this exogamy favors Swahili, which then becomes the children's native tongue. In the urban centers, the situation now favors shift.

Tanzania represents a case where the ultimate loyalty is to the nation, not to the tribe, and so nationalism, of which Swahili is the symbol of *ukuru* and freedom of oppression, is able to support an indigenous language as its official language. In contrast, in Kenya — as in much of Sub-Sahara Africa — the ultimate loyalty lies with the ethnic group, and so nationalism is subsumed under tribal loyalty. In this situation English becomes a neutral language which favors no ethnic group and so becomes the safe official language.

Peru

> Neither a law nor an educational policy can change the social reality of a country, but they can undoubtedly open the way for fundamental changes in the structure of society, thereby making it more amenable to the idea of greater access to material goods and rights in the contemporary world. (Escobar, 1988:388)

Peru represents a case of unsuccessful choice and implementation of an indigenous language as official language (co-equal with Spanish) in Latin America. The military revolutionary government of General Velasco Alvarado designated Quechua as an official language in a Decree Law 21156 of May 27, 1975, but it remained basically only a law on paper, which even so only lasted four years when it was overturned (along with Velasco) in 1979 in the present constitution. The present constitution declares Spanish as the only official language of the nation but recognizes Quechua and Aymara as languages which may be used officially.

Peru is a country of three zones (and cultures): the *costa*, the *sierra*, and the *selva*; coast, mountains, and jungle, the latter two frequently instances of great geographic isolation. There is considerable contrast between the urban and the rural population where, as Escobar points out, the rural is linked with "Indianness," while urban is associated with modernism. The population in 1981 was 17,515,000 of which 65.1% were urban and 34.9 rural. These figures were almost reversed from the 1940 national census which showed 64.5% to be rural of the 6,208,000 population. We see then a country which has experienced considerable population growth and also urbanization as a result of internal migration (primarily to Lima, the capital), but the point Escobar makes is that "it has not caused the sudden conversion of a basically rural country with few urban nuclei in the interior into an urbanized, modern, and homogeneous land that has shaken the symptoms of cultural plurality and provincial multilingualism" (1988:380). There are many ethnic groups and subgroups in Peru, but the basic stratification is between the superordinate Hispanic culture and the subordinate Indian culture, of which the most important and numerous are the Quechua (2-3 million) and Aymara (265,000; figures are from Kloss and McConnell, 1979). Census taking in the sierra and the selva has inherent notorious difficulties, and the figures are best thought of as approximations).

History may give us some insights into why Peru could not do what Tanzania succeeded in. The Quechua-speaking Inca empire was invaded, conquered, and colonized by Pizarro and the Spanish in the 16th century. The main goal held by the Spanish for the Indians was castellanization which had two aspects: learning Spanish and becoming Christianized. But the priests in the early days found it more efficient to spread the word of God in the indigenous language (cf. Swahili) and in fact used Quechua which they helped spread across the empire (Heath and Laprade, 1982). The then king Philip II actually supported the use of the indigenous language.

Opposition came later from priests from Spain who claimed creole (*'born in Peru'*) priests had an unfair advantage. Eventually the policy became to teach and preach in Spanish, and besides interventionist groups like the Summer Institute of Linguistics (North American Protestant missionaries) any other policy has never really been generally implemented. There have been noble attempts, as in the Revolution of 1968 and its Education Reform with its National Bilingual Education Policy of 1972. "The intention of the Reform was to create an educational system that would build up the Peruvian nation along humanistic, democratic and nationalistic lines" (Hornberger, 1985:52). The objectives (about which there was considerable disagreement among the intellectuals) of the Bilingual Education Policy as summarized by Hornberger were (1) consciousness-raising, (2) the creation of a national culture, and (3) the use of Spanish as the common language in Peru (1985:61). Another way of interpretation is to see the policy as an attempt to mobilize the population in a feeling of nationalism along the lines of Haugen's internal cohesion-external distinction (Haugen, 1966).

Quechua has a number of different dialects, some mutually unintelligible, and six varieties were officially standardized after it was declared an official language in 1975. Certainly this variation carried problems of implementation, but one recalls that Swahili also has a number of dialects. Rather the basic problem lay in what it meant to speak Quechua, and in fact the promulgation was never implemented.

Peru was colonized by men with much fewer women than was the case with North America, and the result was widespread miscegenation, so that most Peruvians not of recent external migration are racially mixed or mestizo, which is to say that most are part (or all) Indian in origin. But race is not defined by caste as we tend to do, but rather by social class and culture, of which language is an integral part.

With starched hat, braids and long wide skirts, and a community-centered world view expressed in Quechua, you are an Indian. But go to the city, cut off your hair and wear European style clothing, and accept in Spanish a Latin egocentric world view, and you become mestizo. In fact, it is a very arduous but common process, usually taking two to three generations (Patch, 1967). Typically only the Indian and a few scholars of the upper class will admit to knowing Quechua; for the slowly growing middle class, where you find the public school teachers and the administrators, the Indian heritage is still too uncomfortably close.

In other words, embracing Quechua is to announce to the world that you are Indian, a word so stigmatized in Peruvian Spanish that its official euphemism now is *campesino* 'peasant'. Clearly, any nationalistic fervor, any "internal cohesion-external distinction" rallying around Quechua, such as Swahili has served Tanzania, could not be supported if the pre-condition meant self-identification as an Indian.

Sweden

> Nonetheless, the claim as to Sweden's ethnic homogeneity is not totally unfounded. Compared with a number of European and other countries, the majority population of Sweden is composed primarily of one ethnic group with few foreign elements. (Hyltenstam and Arnberg, 1988:275)

Sweden is an example of a country which has experienced a great deal of recent voluntary migration. At a world standard, Sweden is a very old nation marked until recently by convergent homogeneity of culture and language.[16] Ask any Swede what the traditional Thursday supperdish is, and he will tell you peasoup and pancakes, and indeed it is a rare cafeteria which won't serve it on Thursday. Into this kind of homogeneity of seven million inhabitants came one million immigrants (it much improved the quality of Swedish cuisine) following World War II, primarily during the sixties and seventies; some were refugees,[17] but the majority represented labor market immigration, of which the largest groups came from Yugoslavia, Greece, and Turkey (Hyltenstam and Arnberg, 1988:476), cultures very divergent from Swedish.

The notion of *Gast Arbeiter* 'guest worker' never did exist in Sweden as it did in much of the rest of Europe (meaning the workers were eventually supposed to return home), and a 1975 Parliament Bill established the well-known three official objectives for immigrant and ethnic minorities: (1) equality between immigrants and Swedes; (2) cultural freedom of choice for immigrants; and (3) cooperation and solidarity between Swedes and ethnic minorities. In 1977, the Home Language Reform made it the responsibility of municipalities "to provide home language instruction for all students who desire it and for whom the home language represents a living element in the child's home environment" (Hyltenstam and Arnberg, 1988:488). One can hardly imagine a more idyllic, socialist, positive support for immigrants to maintain their original mother tongue. In fact, it is not happening. Liljegren's data on the home language pupils (those who elect the study of their mother tongue) in Grade 9 document the shift to Swedish which is taking place (1981:30-31). An amazing 94% of children both of whose parents were born in Sweden *always* speak Swedish with either of the parents. Even with parents both of whom were born abroad, one-third (32% of 2,422) of the children *always* speak Swedish at home with at least one parent while an additional 20 *often* do. We see then that among Grade 9 pupils who immigrated before 1970 or were born in Sweden, by the time they have completed compulsory schooling half of them always or often speak Swedish at home with their parents who were born abroad. It is not a complete shift at this point, since the children still maintain the original mother tongue sufficiently for school studies, but that situation is most unlikely to last past another generation or at the most two (Paulston, 1982:38).

The exceptions to language shift (and variable degree of cultural assimilation) are the Rom or gypsies and the Finns.

The gypsies came out of India about the time of Alexander the Great (d. 323 BC) and have for more than 2000 years maintained their Indic language Romani, maybe as a function of the discrimination that they have commonly suffered for their perceived anti-social behavior, cultural behavior at deviance with their host-culture. Clearly gypsy behavior is deviant from Swedish cultural behavior and clearly Swedes discriminate (Trankell, 1974, 1981; Westin, 1981). Both sets of behavior, gypsy cultural behavior and Swedish discriminatory behavior, will tend to enforce ethnic boundary maintenance (Barth, 1969). The Rom no doubt have equality before the law in Sweden, but their situation points out that freedom of choice really only means freedom to choose between alternatives which are acceptable to Swedes. To choose not to send children to compulsory school is simply not an acceptable choice, however appropriate to gypsy culture. As Westin puts it: "the decisive question is whether Swedish society in reality can be ethnically and culturally pluralistic, if a tolerance is possible..." (1981:225). In short, I believe the gypsies will remain gypsies, just as I believe the great-grandchildren of the Estonians and the Hungarians will become Swedes.

The situation of the Finns is theoretically troublesome. They are the single largest immigrant group and constitute about half of the pupil population with a home language other than Swedish. We know that demographic figures are important for language maintenance, but there are other factors as well. Similar to the Puerto Rican situation in the United States, there is considerable back migration and even back and forth migration between Finland and Sweden. Such continued interruption in medium of instruction has negative consequences in the language development of children, although the data we have is basically anecdotal. Certainly the Puerto Rican children's poor school achievement in New York is well attested to. The Finns in Sweden seem to be fairly solidly working class (Steen, 1980:133) with little aspiration for upward social mobility, using such indicators as continued education and job selection (Liljegren, 1982). Interrupted schooling with language change, working class milieu and sometimes low verbal input because of working parents, give cause for concern about children's language development. The Finnish data (Kuusinen, Lasonen, Särkelä, 1977; Toukomaa and Skutnabb-Kangas, 1977; Lasonen and Toukamaa, 1978; Toukomaa and Lasonen, 1970) consistently show the Finnish immigrant children behind the national Finnish norms.[18]

There is another factor which differentiates the Finns from the other immigrants, and that is a matter of nationalism. We seek to understand all the other immigrant groups in Sweden from a perspective of ethnicity, ethnic groups as categories of ascription and identification which share "fundamental cultural values, realized in overt unity in cultural forms" (Barth, 1969:11) and usually a common language. The freedom of choice really concerns a freedom for individual immigrants to choose just how much they want to maintain their original ethnic boundaries or cross over into Swedish culture. What the Finns want is not ethnic boundary maintenance but rather extended nationalism (see e.g. Similä, 1980). Nationalism does not concern the choice of individuals but the rights of the group. It is not at all clear how united the Finnish group is in its goal for maintained Finnish nationalism in Sweden. Of Liljegren's Finnish 9th graders, 53% speak Swedish always (36%) or often (17%) with their parents[19], which situation looks like one of incipient shift. Whatever decisions need to be made are clearly political in nature and would only marginally have to do with language, were it not for the situation of back and forth migration. The Swedish guideline has been one of equal treatment for all immigrants, and in this context I would merely like to point out the rationale for bilingual education as seen by the United States Supreme Court: equal treatment does not constitute equal opportunity. Of the immigrant groups, the Finns probably best stand to profit by bilingual education.

In my 1982 report to the National Swedish Board of Education (NBE) on *Swedish Research and Debate about Bilingualism*, I pointed out that some topics are uniquely Swedish. I want to repeat my comments here about semilingualism as I occasionally see the topic resurfacing in odd corners of the world.

The notion of semilingualism was popularized in Sweden with the publication of Hansegård's *Tvåspråkighet eller halvspråkighet?* (Bilingualism or Semilingualism) in 1968, but Ekstrand's (1981: 45ff.) account of its previous history sounds credible. The term had its roots in the Finnish language struggle, surfaced in print in the press and always was a layman's term and never a theoretical concept. The term, as any Swede will know, refers to the imperfect learning of two languages, or to cite the Immigrant Bureau's in Stockholm (Invandrarexpeditionen) *Invandrarundervisningen i Stockholms skolor* (The Education of Immigrants in Stockholm Schools, 1979:11): "a poor Swedish which unfortunately laid the foundation for what we call semilingualism" or the Local Education Authority in Lund: "The compulsory crash course in Swedish resulted in semilingualism for many immigrant children..." (Anderson et al. 1980:11). The fact of the matter is that there is *no* empirical evidence to support the existence of such a language development hiatus as Hansegård claims. Linguist after linguist in Sweden (Hyltenstam and Stroud, 1982; Loman, 1974; Martin-Jones and Romaine, 1987; Oksaar, 1980; Stolt, 1975; Stroud, 1978; Stroud and Wingstedt, 1989; Wande, 1977; Öhman, 1981) has criticized the notion. Loman specificaly looked for evidence and found none. Nor did Ekvall (1979) or Nystål and Sjöberg (1976) or Rönmark and Wikström (1980).

The widespread mythology of semilingualism when there are no data is astounding to the outsider. Such mythology has obviously served a purpose: people believe what they want to. It has served as rationale for the Finnish (again) groups in their demands for monolingual Finnish schooling in Sweden. It has also served as a rationale for the Swedish parents in Södertälje who do not want the Assyrian children in the same classes as their own children (Field notes, March 1982). There is anecdotal evidence that most immigrant parents wanted their children in mixed Swedish classes until they were informed about the dangers of semilingualism. In Hilmerson et al.'s study, 61% of the Greek parents "consider that there is a risk for semilingualism if their children do not receive home language instruction" (1980:14). It is preferable to segregate children on the basis of preventing harm, i.e. semilingualism, than on the basis of racial discrimination, at least in Sweden.

In my conclusions to that report I made the following comments, which I still find valid and which illustrate my notion that in matters of language and ethnicity, language only becomes important in adverse situations, not the case in Sweden. The key question, as I see it, is well recognized if phrased variously:

> But yet there are no research results in the immigration countries which indicate whether the establishment of (migrant) national schools supports or hinders the children's long range possibilities to

> find jobs or social conditions which are equal to those of other children. (Widgren, 1981:11)

or more tersely

> How do you achieve a society where each individual has social equality with maintained cultural freedom of choice and identity (NBE, 1979:107).

Given these facts:

1. The immigrant children do as well in school as the Swedish children[20] (Liljegren, 1981; Petersen, n.d.,Wennerström, 1967).
2. The immigrant children demonstrate a strong tendency to shift to Swedish.
3. The Swedish population shows strong xenophobic inclinations. Svenska Dagbladet (1980) reports that parents in Botkyrka have requested monolingual Swedish classes, i.e. without any immigrant children. When I asked the Assyrian teacher in Södertälje whether his students (in a mother tongue class speaking primarily Swedish) at least had physical education and music with the Swedish children, he told me that they used to, but the Swedish parents had complained to the headmaster that the Assyrian children were too 'rowdy' so they discontinued that practice. (Fieldnotes, March 1982)
4. Immigrant children's special teachers tend to be untrained in mother tongue teaching as well as in Swedish as a foreign language. Tingbjörn refers to the "absence of regularized teacher education" (Tingbjörn, 1981:13) as one of remarkable lags, as well he might. In a school I visited, every one of the nine Turkish teachers chose to put their own children in regular Swedish classes.
5. Many if not most proponents for mother tongue teaching have a vested interest in the maintained lack of assimilation of migrant children. This fact does not automatically invalidate the opin-

ions of this group, but their lack of objectivity is marked, and their advice vis-à-vis educational language policy needs to be considered *cum grano salis*. They will strenuously object to this point and instead point out that no one is as familiar with the problems of migrant children as they are. This point is also true and needs to be considered.
6. Semilingualism does not exist, or put in a way which is non-refutable, has never been empirically demonstrated.

It seems that common sense alone would come to the following conclusion: any decent interpretation of freedom of choice must support the children in their voluntary assimilation with combined classes, which they themselves find important (Petersen, n.d.:4), strong auxiliary teaching (Jelonek, 1975), and a strong support of Swedish as a foreign language (Sfs). The demands for mother tongue classes almost invariably come from parents, parents' groups and immigrant organizations but not from the children (with the exception of older arrivals who do not have the alternative option of adequate Sfs training). Mother tongue classes are partly an excuse, a mechanism for segregation, which happens to coincide with Finnish national demands, and therefore meets with Finnish support. Mother tongue instruction is nice and makes possible a recognition of the values of the old country. As a linguist, I am very much in favour of it and recognize Swedish educational policy of mother tongue instruction as a very handsome gesture of the Swedish government. It is also a very expensive policy (about 230 million Sw crowns in governmental grant, 1983/84) and in the Swedish case, only indispensible for linguistic minority groups with a record of back migration.

Since then, costs have increased and the estimate is that between the school years 1982-83 and 1988-89, they increased by 21 percent. In 1991, the total federal expenditures on the education of immigrants and their children were said to be at one milliard crowns

(10^9) (Hyltenstam, 1991). There is slight wonder then at the government's serious attempts in poor economic times to cut down on the costs and the programs themselves. The National Board of Education has been abolished and more responsibility turned over to the local communes, which are likely to be less willing and less able to support expensive home language teaching.

Hyltenstam suggests that the ethnic groups in Sweden who wish to maintain their language and culture take responsibility for their own childrens' education (1991:7). I agree with him that in a shift situation such as in Sweden, it is probably the only way to maintain the groups' original ethnic mother tongue. We have seen it with the Jews throughout the ages, and this maintained knowledge of written Hebrew made possible the revival of Hebrew to become the national language of Israel. It is likely to be the lesson from the Maori of New Zealand as well. The real question is whether the immigrant children will accept being separated from mainstream Swedish schooling. It is a high price to pay for being able to speak your grandfather's language, and I doubt that it will happen except for maybe the Finns.

Analysis and Discussion

I discussed in the preceding chapter a theoretical framework for explaining and predicting the language behavior of ethnic groups in contact within a contemporary nation-state and will here examine the case studies in light of this framework. The proposition is that linguistic groups form four distinct types of social mobilization: ethnicity, ethnic movements, ethnic nationalism and geographic nationalism which under certain specified social conditions result in differential linguistic outcomes of language maintenance and shift.

There is in fact little power struggle and not much purpose with ethnicity, and so the common course is assimilation and concomitant language shift. Ethnicity will not maintain a language in a multilingual setting if the dominant group allows assimilation, and incentive and opportunity of access to the national language are present. The immigrant groups to Sweden (with the exception of the Finns) are a very good example of this point. Voluntary migration, access to public schools and thus to the national language, and economic incentives in the form of available jobs all contribute to assimilation and language shift. I have earlier discussed other factors as well, like low Swedish tolerance for culture differences. The very liberal Swedish educational language policies of mother tongue instruction will not succeed in bringing about mother tongue maintenance and will at most contribute to a few generations of bilingualism before complete shift to Swedish.

The Indian groups of Peru is another example of ethnicity and language shift within a nation-state. The shift is infinitely slower than in Sweden, and we can identify such factors as colonization, much less economic incentive and more difficulty in access to Spanish because of geographic isolation which contribute to that slower shift. We also need to consider the stigmatized status of things Indian and the cultural definition of race. The rewards clearly lie within Hispanic culture, and under these conditions General Velasco's language policies of bilingual education and Quechua as an official language clearly failed in stirring up national consciousness, in bringing about a sense of nationalism.

The major difference between ethnicity and ethnic movement is when ethnicity as an unconscious source of identity turns into a conscious strategy, usually in competition for scarce resources.

Ethnic movements by themselves probably cannot maintain a language but will effect rate of shift, so that the shift is much slower and spans many more generations. None of these case studies exemplify an ethnic movement. Peru does have *Sendero Luminoso*, the terrorist Maoist Shining Path movement, but its leadership is university educated and functions in Spanish. More importantly, their claims are not drawn along ethnic boundaries but rather along social class.

Shafer concludes that it is impossible to fit nationalism into a short definition (1972:5), but I have attempted to identify some salient features: Group cohesion to the end, goal-orientation of self-determination, a perceived threat of opposing forces and access to or hope of territory are characteristics of all national movements.

In ethnic or closed nationalism the ethnic group is isomorphic with the nation-state. The emphasis is on the nation's autochthonous character, on the common origin and ancestral roots. Finland is an example of ethnic nationalism, and I have frequently heard it remarked in Sweden that Finns are much more nationalistic than Swedes. As I have commented, the demands for Finnish linguistic rights, made not so much by the immigrants themselves as by official Finnish organizations, is best understood as an expression of nationalism rather than ethnicity.

As we saw in the preceding chapter, Catalunya exemplifies a nation with sustained language maintenance in spite of prohibition and prosecution. The monolingual Spanish medium schools were not successful in bringing about shift from Catalan to Spanish although they were successful in establishing widespread bilingualism. The educational language policies were not successful because they went counter to the prevailing social forces of strong economic incentives and geographic nationalism and stubborn pride, all of which favored the maintenance of Catalan.

Tanzania on the other hand is a case of highly successful language policies, both choice of national language and choice of medium of instruction. I have earlier listed a number of reasons for this success, but ultimately the most explanatory factor lies in the unusual African situation that most Tanzanians identify first as Tanzanian and only second as member of a tribe (I have heard them speak very derogatorily about the exceptions), i.e. successful language policies as a function of geographic nationalism. The major social institution for the spread of Swahili has been the public schools, and probably also the Armed Forces. Along the coast, urbanization also contributes to the successful implementation of Swahili.

All of these cases illustrate in various ways that ethnic minority groups within a nation state will shift to the national language, given opportunity and incentive. Only a (strong) sense of nationalism will maintain a minority language. For Tanzania, nationalism does not make possible the maintenance of the ethnic language but rather the bilingualism of the ethnic language — and so maintenance — with the acceptance of an indigenous language as the nation's official language. Tanzanians are willing to accept the primacy of the state over tribal affiliations, and so are one of the few African nations with an official indigenous language which *in fact* serves as the national language.

Chapter 6

Language Revitalization

The Case of Irish

Introduction

This chapter examines present day language planning efforts in Ireland in order to further explore the theoretical framework discussed in chapter 3 to allow us to explain and to predict the language behavior of groups who have access to or are exposed to more than one language. I consider such an understanding vital to helpful educational policies and to succesful language planning in general.

I have claimed that ethnicity and ethnic movements are not sufficiently supportive types of social mobilization to maintain ethnic languages, but that some form of nationalism seems necessary to maintain the language of linguistic minorities within a nation-state, or indeed, even to maintain the language of a recent majority as in Ireland.

Language planning in Ireland is not a new endeavor. Status planning, i.e. planning concerning language policies, is well in place. With the establishment of the Irish Free State in 1922, Irish was declared the national and first official language. Educational policies are generally accepted with Irish being taught in the primary schools and as an optional subject in the secondary. Corpus planning, planning the linguistic forms of the language such as standardization of the grammar and the lexicon, has also been in place since the late fifties, based primarily on the Connacht Irish dialect (Macnamara, 1971:73-74).

Rather, the concern is with language revitalization. This concern goes far back in Irish history, but in recent times the main center of such language planning efforts is the Bord na Gaeilge, established by the government in 1978 for the promotion of Irish. An Coiste Comhairleach Pleanala (The Advisory Planning Committee) of the Bord na Gaeilge in 1988 published their second report, entitled *The Irish Language in a Changing Society: Shaping the Future* (ILCS). This report on the Irish language situation documents the shift to English and suggests strategies for reversing the situation. It is primarily these strategies or remedies I wish to discuss in this chapter.

Background

The Irish people were originally Irish Gaelic (mostly referred to as simply Irish) speaking with a culture (and later a literature) that goes back over a thousand years. The Anglo-Norman invasion of 1172 overturned the traditional life of the country even though the early settlers seem to have shifted to Irish, except within the Pale. As Edwards writes:

> The Statutes of Kilkenny (1366) demonstrate the power of Irish and the apprehension of the threat it posed to English. The thirty-six regulations (written incidentally in Norman French — a telling indicator of linguistic realities) were intended to keep English settlers from adapting Irish ways, and covered everything from speaking in English to riding in the English manner. (1984: 268)

By the 17th century English rule was oppressively in place and a gradual shift to English, increasingly the language of status and power, began. By 1851, when the first census to take account of language was held, only 5% of the population identified themselves as monolingual Irish speakers (Macnamara, 1971: 65), and today all native Irish speakers are bilingual. (CLAR, 1975: 3) The present percentage of native speakers of Irish varies with the source; Fasold claims that the 1961 census indicates that between two to three percent of the population are native speakers (1984:278), while ILCS states:

> Recent surveys would suggest the proportion who use Irish as their first or main language to be something around 5%, but because the use of Irish changes over the life-cycle of individual bilinguals, the proportion who at some time in their lives used Irish relatively intensively might be 15%. A further 10% or so of the population use Irish regularly but less intensively in conversation or reading. As opposed to these relatively low ratios of spoken or active use of Irish, the ratios of passive use, primarily listening/watching Irish language radio and television programmes are considerably higher. About 25% of the population watch some Irish language program weekly and up to 70% watch such programmes at least occasionally. These levels of use clearly suggest that there is a reservoir of bilingual potential in the community which is not being realized in spoken use. (1988:32)

And that is exactly what the report identifies as the basic problem: in spite of the educational policies of teaching Irish to all school children, English is primarily spoken. "The central problem, however, is that popular use of the language (Irish) has remained at a low level and current indications are that there is contracting further in some important respects" (ILCS, 1988:x).

Language Planning Efforts

In spite of a number of government involvements[21] aimed at restoring the Irish language, the present situation is one of a very far gone language shift; indeed, as the first seven chapters of the ILCS report predict, the disappearance of Irish as a living language is a very likely possibility. (Presumably the symbolic importance of Irish will continue so it will continue to be studied and learned much as Latin has been for centuries.)

What efforts then are being undertaken to halt this situation? Bord na Gaeilge in its 1989 report *Key to the Future of the Irish Language* (KFIL) introduces itself as the state language planning authority to express and link state policy with all groups involved with Irish. "The Bord is language planner, catalyst and co-ordinator in its task of developing a bilingual Ireland" (1989:3). It lists as its objectives: (1) to plan, guide and deploy the appropriate resources for the implementation of a comprehensive strategy for the creation of an effectively bilingual society in Ireland by the end of the century, and (2) to further develop public support for the view that some ability in speaking Irish is a key factor in Irish identity (1989:5), reflecting the two social functions of the Irish language: communicative and symbolic. They identify seven strategies to do this: central planning, state and public leadership for real impact, expand networks and structures of usage, increase the visibility of Irish, ensure service through Irish in the Gaeltacht, a teaching revolution (new syllabi and methods), and innovative communications, like radio and TV programs, and newsletters.

Among Bord na Gaeilge's listed achievements, resulting from their *Action Plan for 1983-86,* are the increased number of All-Irish school and playgroups, increasing Irish proficiency of trainee teachers, broadcasting in Irish increased, developing a planning framework which involved other organizations and rekindled interest, and making the proposed bilingual objective clear to the public.

The Bord also lists as an achievement its Advisory Planning Committee's publication of *The Irish Language in a Changing Society* which it points out "has been acclaimed as the most important analysis and assessment of the language to date" (1989:11). It quotes the 1988 report:

> The fact is that Irish, by far the less widely spoken of Ireland's two languages, appears to be highly valued by the majority of the population as a symbol of Irish identity and of the separateness of its people. What is needed now is clear public realization of the central goals and strategies that must be pursued in order, at least, to halt the current drift and ideally, to translate passive ideological support into greater ability...and this greater ability into usage.
>
> Both state and voluntary effort continue to be needed, to formulate and implement policies which would extend and secure usage.
>
> Current needs
> 1. to refashion a new concept of modern Irish identity incorporating an ideological rationale for Irish,
> 2. a popular cultural movement and,
> 3. the state to assume an active role in fulfilling its own declared commitments to the language.
>
> It appears to be at the level of usage that the most intensive policy efforts are now needed (1989:11).

Discussion

Basically I think that the Irish language planning efforts are doomed to failure. These are my reasons.

The very goal of "the creation of an effectively bilingual society" (Bord na Gaeilge, 1989:5) is unrealistic. Group bilingualism, given incentive to shift, is unusual. As I have stated earlier, the norm for groups in prolonged contact within one nation is for the subordinate group to shift to the language of the dominant group, either over several hundred years as with Gaelic in Great Britain and Ireland, or over the span of three generations as with the European immigrants to the United States.

The mechanism of language shift is bilingualism, often but not necessarily so with exogamy, where parent(s) speak(s) the original language with the grandparents and the new language with the children. Many Gaeltacht[22] parents now choose to bring their children up in English and many out-migrating young men and women marry monolingual English speakers.

Language shift is often considered as an indicator of cultural assimilation, of loss of the values of the original culture. ILCS does consider Irish as a marker of cultural identity. However, there is no isomorphic relationship between language and culture, nor is language maintenance necessary for culture and ethnicity maintenance. The report claims that "the Irish language has an integral and creative role to play in a modern definition of Irish identity" (1988:91). Certainly it could play such a role, but my point is that in the likely absence of the Irish language, Irish identity can be just as strongly defined through the medium of English. After all, Synge and Yeats and Joyce wrote in English and none will deny their Irish identity.

We know that the major linguistic consequence of ethnic groups in prolonged contact within one nation is language shift, but what is less understood (really not studied at all) is the degree to which such groups keep their communicative competence rules and apply their own cultural rules of appropriate language use to the new language. How Irishly do the Irish behave in English? We know virtually nothing about this aspect of language shift, but it is easy to speculate that a slow shift as in Ireland is more likely to guard cultural ways of using language. Indeed, ILCS remarks on the aping of English styles by yuppie (not the report terminology) Irishmen.

This shift only takes place if there is (1) opportunity and (2) incentive for the group to learn the national language. Henry VIII clearly saw the need for opportunity to learn and ordered the Irish children to school in order to learn English. The National School system, established in 1831, was called the 'murder machine' of Irish (Edwards, 1985:54). The two major kinds of incentive are economic advantage and social prestige, and both have been and are at work in Ireland. One third of the manufacturing is owned by outside multinational corporations, and as a member of EEC, Ireland is discouraged by economic forces from intensive ethnic boundary maintenance. Also, through modernization and industrialization of the economic scene, social prestige has changed from ascribed to achieved status, in which Irish plays no part. All social factors argue for complete shift to the dominant English language.

Where shift does not take place, it is for three major reasons, and none now are salient in Ireland.

1. Self-imposed boundary maintenance, always for reasons other than language, most frequently religion as with the Amish. Irish serves no particular religious function as does Hebrew, nor did the Catholic Church serve as a unified defender of Irish as she did in Catalunya for Catalan. (There were of course individual priests who did.) The Catholic Church turned to English, and Irish became associated with Protestant proselytizing societies.

> The general view seemed to be that it was better to save souls than Irish and, as priests were often managers of primary schools the language was often actively discouraged there (O'Donnell, 1903). (Edwards, 1985:54).

2. Externally imposed boundaries, usually in the form of denied access to goods and services, especially jobs. Historically such boundary maintenance existed as in the Statutes of Kilkenny which had the effect of excluding the Irish from the Pale, but at that time Irish was strong. Today, the economic market encourages English. Geographic isolation is also a form of external boundary which contributes to language maintenance. As *ILCS* points out: "Irish has survived in the Gaeltactai largely because they were economically and geographically peripheral areas" (1988:1).

3. A diglossic-like (Ferguson, 1959) situation where the two languages exist in a situation of functional distribution, in which each language has its specified purpose and domain, and the one language is inappropriate in the other situation. *ILCS* discusses the network versus the domain model of bilingualism and is

quite convincing in its documentation of the network model for Irish usage, which it predicts is likely to lead to shift or more exactly the non-maintenance of Irish.[23]

Current Needs

Ideological rationale for Irish *ILCS* argues that a priority for Irish language planning is a restatement of "an authoritative, ideological rationale for defending and taking pride in the language" (1988:91). They point out that Irish is highly valued by the majority as a symbol of Irish identity and claim that it is because Irish has served this function that the country has remained, to a degree, a bilingual society. At the same time, elsewhere in the report, they cite the Directors of CLAR, Brudner and White:

> Language attitudes in Ireland, while highly structured, internally coherent, and superficially correlated with language usage, do not appear to exert any independent effect on the individual's own language behaviour (1979:65).

In other words, people may perceive of Irish as having a very high symbolic value for the nation, without at the same time being willing or able to use it in daily discourse.

While the report is searching for an ideological rationale for Irish, it denies the need for nationalism. "Irish peoplehood would be expressed in a universalist rather than particularistic or insular terms. This means not so much affirming an Irishness because of singularly Irish characteristics, but doing so in a way that would contribute positively to the evolution of the community of nations" (1988:92). Not surprisingly, the report continues with a disclaimer that it cannot undertake the task of outlining such a modern philosophy of Irishness, but that they feel it essential for the establishment of a bilingual society. The report is absolutely right in seeing the need to motivate the people to want to take the trouble to learn and use Irish, but Irish identity and modern philosophy will not provide that motivation. They also tie the ideological rationale to motivating the generation of a popular cultural movement.

A Popular Cultural Movement

ILCS calls for a populist cultural movement, mobilized around conceptions about a modern Irish identity. "If it were sufficiently attractive, particularly to young people, it could help to diffuse hostility to the language and encourage the translation of speaking ability into usage" (1988:94). What they are calling for is a form of social mobilization strong enough to carry a revitalization of Irish. In my previous discussion on linguistic consequences for ethnic groups in multilingual settings, I identified four types of social mobilization: ethnicity, ethnic movement, ethnic nationalism, and geographic nationalism.

Ireland is in a bind. Of these four types of social mobilization only nationalism is strong enough to work for maintenance or revival. However, it is an unavoidable fact that nationalism as a social phenomenon is a stigmatized behavior in present day EEC Europe for reasons of historical events during the last century. As I have pointed out earlier, there is strong hesitation to again encourage nationalism. The report frequently alludes to the Canadian situation as a model. The reversal of the language shift situation in Quebec is a clear case of nationalism to the point of separatism, where the adversity toward the Anglo population is the rallying cry for the Francophones. A perceived threat of opposing forces is a defining characteristic of most if not all national movements. Today Ireland lacks that sense of urgency for language survival.

Another case frequently alluded to is the case of Catalan where language legislation is cited as a causal factor for its maintenance. But the very same legislation has done nothing to halt the shift to

Spanish for Gallego and Basque within the same nation. Rather, the cause for maintenance of Catalan has little to do with legislation and is instead due to the dominant economic situation and deep-seated nationalism of Catalunya as discussed in chapter 4. In short, without a very urgent sense of nationalism, I doubt that any cultural movement based on 'modern philosophy' will have any chance for maintaining, less creating the use of Irish.

The State to Assume an Active Role

ICLS encourages state intervention in three areas: (1) legal and administrative changes, (2) infrastructural provisioning and planning and (3) the social organization of Irish usage.

The report calls for the development and legislation to secure equal legal status of Irish and English. Although Article 8 of the Constitution sets out the constitutional standing of both official languages, it does not detail practical legislative provision, and in fact the current standing of Irish is dependent on case law rather than on legislation (1988:93). They clearly see the problems. "While, in theory, state directives on policy are conceivable, the reality is that a certain level of popular consensus about the aims of policy is essential if policy measures are not to cause public resentment" (1988:93). Status language planning in a democracy does demand popular consensus or at least a majority consensus, or the party will be voted out of power. Countries which have successfully used legislation to enforce language choice like Algeria (from French to Modern Standard Arabic) and Tanzania (from English to Swahili) have been one party nations. Even then, the social conditions favored such a choice, including a strong sense of nationalism.

The report mentions another very interesting point about legislative provision. Legislation inevitably interprets rights as attaching to individuals rather than to groups or collectivities:

> A point worth bearing in mind here is the ineffectiveness of much legislation which is couched in terms of individual rights, when it encounters threat to a good which is common rather than individual. A pertinent example would appear to be the laws governing planning applications by non-Irish speakers to build houses in existing Gaeltacht areas. Under the law, neither the objectives of Gaeltacht policy, nor the threat to the survival of the minority language community, can be used as legitimate objections to such applications. Individual rights take precedence over a common good. (1988:95)

The real question, for which I have no answer, would seem to be: What does it take to mobilize popular will so that it supports legislation enforcing the use of Irish? Given a choice between, on the one hand, economic well-being through instrumental use of English and, on the other, ideological use of Irish, most Irish already seem to have made that choice, and consequently legislation is of not much use.

The basic principle of infrastructural planning demands that all state agencies be able to use Irish and that there be "no barriers to the use of Irish by the general public in interacting with any of the major public service departments or agencies, in particular health, social welfare, education, training, environment and agriculture" (1988:96). It seems a sensible demand similar to Canadian legislation, but in practice it does not work. The basic principle of language choice in encounters between individuals is quite theoretically uninteresting: you select that language in which both have the best proficiency. I speak English with my husband because my English is better than his Swedish, a totally practical matter. Similarly, if a Gaeltacht peasant, bilingual since birth, goes to an agricultural agency for help and meets an anglophone agent who studied Irish in school ten years ago, it would be totally unnatural for them to speak Irish. This is the reason for the CLAR report finding, cited in *ILCS* (1988:99), that "even in designated Irish sections of Departments," Irish was rarely, if ever, spoken in the course of the work (1975:345).

Under the heading of Social Organization of Irish Usage, the report calls for the State to become involved in active promotion and organization of use. They point out that in recent years the State increasingly regulates social and cultural as well as economic organizations, mostly by the provision of public money. This function could be used to encourage the recipients to enhance the use of Irish. There could also be institutional parallelism in such social domains as taxation, social welfare and education. They also call for "positive discrimination" in the forms of capitation grants to schools and extra resources to all-Irish schools.

This brings up another difficulty with the proposed strategies. Official bilingualism with parallel institutions for a country like Ireland where all speak English is an expensive undertaking. The Bord na Gaeilge 1989 report calls for a yearly budget of 1,030,000 pounds (US$1,514,100.00), excluding the expenses of teaching Irish in the public schools. There is of course no price on national pride and identity, and it is for the Irish people to decide how they spend their money. However, given the highly unlikely chance of success, the Irish language planning efforts seem excessively costly, not only in money but in time and energy. But while the Irish may lack—or already have achieved and left behind,—the characteristics of nationalism, there is no denying their strong sense of ethnic identity, and while Irish may disappear as a spoken language, the likelihood is strong that no cost will be considered too high to maintain its symbolic value and existence.

Chapter 7

Language Regenesis

Language Revival, Revitalization and Reversal

(With Pow Chee Chen and Mary C. Connerty)

Preface

Strictly speaking, this chapter does not belong in this book. It barely seems to consider the issues discussed earlier. I suppose it could be seen as an outline for another book.

Yet, these are thoughts and concerns which have followed from my earlier work, are solidly based on that work, and may be taken to indicate future directions to be considered in language shift situations. So it seemed to me appropriate to include it here. (C.B.P.)

Introduction

Scholars of the sociology of language have long been concerned with language maintenance and shift and related questions, such as language death and revival. There is considerable conceptual confusion or, more charitably put, a lack of general agreement over what constitutes language revival. The term is frequently used synonymously with language revitalization, and recently Fishman (1990) has introduced the initials RLS (reversing language shift), further adding to the terminology. We will argue in this paper that language revival, language revitalization, and language reversal constitute three separate phenomena, subsumed under the concept of language regenesis. We will define and illustrate language regenesis and its subcategories with the intent of establishing a clear and common terminology for these concepts.

Our approach is basically comparative. We have examined a number of case studies (Catalunya; Faroese/Faroe Islands - Denmark; Finland; Greece; Hebrew/Israel; Indonesia; Ireland; Korea; Kurdish; Maori/New Zealand; Norway; Poland; South Africa; Tanzania), selected either from a general knowledge of the situation or because they appeared as case studies in *The Problem of Language Revival* (Ellis and mac a'Ghobhainn, 1971). We examined these for similarities and differences, looking for defining characteristics and for the conditions under which they occurred. Our aim has been to clarify our understanding of language regenesis as we seek to comprehend, explain and predict the behavior of ethnic groups in their *increased* use of dead, dying, neglected or underutilized languages. Subsumed under language regenesis are, as previously stated, language revival, revitalization and reversal. We intend the literal meaning of language revival; that is, the giving of new life to a dead language, or the act of reviving a language after discontinuance, and making it the normal means of communication in a speech community. By language revitalization, we mean the imparting of new vigor to a language still in limited or restricted use, most commonly by increased use through the expansion of domains. And, finally, by language reversal, we mean the turning around of present trends in a language. We would add that the concept needs to be subdivided into three types, namely legal reversal, reversal of shift, and rebound of an exoglossic language; all of these refer to a "turning around" of present trends of a language, yet each has a specific focus. Legal reversal and reversal of shift often co-occur with (or immediately precede or follow) corpus planning, i.e. planning the linguistic forms of the language such as standardization of the grammar and the lexicon. Any language can, in its historical development, be at various times in a stage of revitalization or in reversal; thus Catalan's legal language reversal after Franco was preceded by language revitalization in the 19th century, with no immediate causal relationship between the two. On the other hand, Tanzanian Swahili had legal reversal after obtaining independence from Britain, followed by language revitalization as a direct result of this reversal.[24]

Language Revival

Thomason (1982) defines a dead language as one which (1) has no native speakers, (2) is not used in everyday communication by a speech community, and (3) does not undergo normal processes of change. Language revival then refers to bringing a dead language back to life. Nahir (1984:301) defines revival as "the attempt to turn a language with few or no surviving native speakers back into a normal means of communication in a community". The only true example of language revival which we find is Hebrew. An ancient language, Hebrew began to decline as early as 586 BC with the removal of a large number, including the upper echelons, of the Jews to Babylon. With the Babylonian exile, Hebrew speakers became bilingual in Aramaic and later Greek, and in the next few hundred years Hebrew disappeared as a spoken means of communication. It remained in use as a written language, used for prayers, study and literacy, both secular and religious.

With the rise of nationalism in the 1800s, anti-Semitism in Europe increased, sometimes with violent consequences; one result was a series of *aliyot,* or waves of immigration, of Jews to Palestine. By the late 1800s, the number of Jews immigrating to Palestine was growing. These people came from various countries and spoke various languages; therefore, a common language was needed for what was to become a new nation.

The notion of reviving Hebrew had begun to grow along with ideas of Jewish national revival in the latter part of the 19th century, when some Jews were persuaded that the modernization and secularization of European society had not ended anti-Semitism. (See Glinert (1991) for an unusual account of the Hebrew revival.) By 1914, the revival of Hebrew was virtually complete. By 1917, when the British took Jerusalem from the Turkish Empire, the Jewish population in Palestine was 56,000, and 34,000 were already speaking Hebrew. Between 1917 and 1948, 576,000 Jews immigrated to Palestine, where, under the British Mandate, English had become an official language together with Arabic and Hebrew. However, the use of Hebrew continued to grow, as did the changes and modernization of the language itself. The majority of Hebrew speakers were in smaller, rural areas and villages. There, they were truly a mix of nationalities and needed a lingua franca to form their communities. For many communities, Yiddish would have been a sensible choice, as most of the settlers were from eastern Europe and already spoke it. However, Yiddish was seen by many as a jargon of the Diaspora and of low prestige. It was resented for being associated with persecution and exile. Moreover, the intensely favorable attitudes towards Hebrew were an integral part of the language's revival. Not only the sacred language of the Torah, it was also the language spoken by the group's forefathers in an ancient and independent homeland and was very much a focus of their social identification. Because most men knew at least the prayers in Hebrew, there was a basis to start.

According to Nahir (1988:281-289), the most important factor in turning Hebrew from a language struggling to be revived into a native language was the children in the rural communities. They were instilled with the desired, positive attitudes towards Hebrew. Then, in special pre-schools, and later in primary and secondary schools, they were presented with and acquired the language from teachers who spoke to them *only* in Hebrew. Because of the positive attitudes, they spoke the language out of school as well and, by the next generation, the newborn children were receiving and speaking Hebrew as their first language. In this way, the language began to grow and change, once again becoming a living, vibrant language and the normal means of communication within the speech community. In effect, the children helped the adults to learn and speak Hebrew, a kind of reverse direction of language learning. These factors, along with the increased popularity of the Hebrew press, the increase in the number of schools, and mandatory military service, all supported the only true example we have found of language revival.

What conditions, then, are associated with an attempt to bring new life to a dead or dying language? First, there must be an old language to be revived, one which reflects the nation's *glorious past.* That is, the old language provides a desired historical, cultural, literary and, perhaps religious, affinity with the original community. Important here are strong feelings of nationalism, whereby a group of individuals begins to see itself as part of a nation-state, sharing common goals, ideals, and the desire for statehood. Language thus becomes an important symbol of their national identity.

Probably the most important condition for language revival is the *need* for a means of communication.[25] There must exist a situation where a community of people have no LWC, need to communicate, and have an "old revivable language" (Nahir, 1988:276) at their disposal which binds them together historically. By *need* we mean more than simply speech; if speech were enough, Yiddish might have sufficed for Israel, or a new pidgin/creole language could have been developed. *Need* includes the pre-existence of sociolinguistic factors (such as historical, political, religious and educational affiliations) which have brought people of different linguistic backgrounds together (Nahir, 1988:276-277).

That vibrant trend of nationalism, which began around the end of the 18th century and which resulted in an increased sense of national identity and independence, has continued to influence numerous language situations. Some of these have been labeled revival. For example, the declaration of Irish as the official language in 1922 by the Irish Free State, and subsequent policies to promote the use of the language, have often been labeled language revival. However, Irish does not meet all of the above criteria for a dead language. That is, Irish has a community of native speakers (albeit a small one), is used in everyday communication by this speech community, and undergoes normal processes of change. In addition, there is no need for an LWC because of the presence of English. By the same token, Welsh has had a successful resurgence, but it too does not qualify as an instance of revival. Never a dead language, Welsh has constantly been changing and evolving. Maori is another group whose language has been termed "revived"; yet there was never a generation without native speakers who kept the language alive.

Today, Hebrew is a vital language which has changed dramatically from the ancient variety the early settlers knew. As an example of language revival, it meets all of the criteria — it had no native speakers, was not used as a common language of communication and was not undergoing any normal processes of change,— i.e. it was a dead language. Moreover, the conditions were right: the need for a LWC and the availability of an old language which had the historical and cultural affinity required by the people to support their desire for nationhood. The historical period in which the revival took place — in which occurred the rise of nationalism and anti-Semitism in Europe — provided a unique series of events in world history which strengthened the need for a Hebrew language. The revival of Hebrew has been referred to as a "historical accident" (Nahir, 1988) and perhaps it was the unique set of historical events which makes Hebrew the only true case of language revival in history as we know it.

Language Revitalization

In contrast to language revival, revitalization does not refer to the rebirth of a dead language, but rather to the new-found vigor of a language already in use. For example, after the rebirth of Hebrew had been firmly established, the language went through major changes in order to modernize (i.e. corpus planning, necessitated by the expansion of domains). Korean, after years of being influenced by Chinese and repressed by the Japanese, became the rallying point around which intellectuals and anti-colonial activists focused their demands for independence. Korean newspapers and magazines played an important role in the spread of the writing system, though it was not until after World War II that Korean became the medium of instruction and the official language of the courts and media. Similarly, in Tanzania there was a movement, after the end of the colonial period, to expand the usage of Swahili so that it could become the language of government and public administration which represents a case of language revitalization.

A clear example of language revitalization can be found with Finnish. Finland came under Swedish domination in the 13th century and remained an integral part of that country until 1809, when it came under Russian rule. Around the middle of the 18th century, a Finnish awareness began to appear. Finns began to complain about the appointment of Swedes to all administrative and judicial posts, and about their lack of knowledge of the Finnish language and customs. With the end of Swedish rule, in 1809, many younger Finnish patriots feared eventual linguistic and political "Russification". The country was divided into two linguistic parts: the Finnish speakers and the Swedish speakers. The overwhelming majority was Finnish speaking, and the young patriots fixed their attention on converting the upper and middle class Swedish speakers to Finnish. The Swedish language had been important because of Finland's subsidiary role in the Swedish kingdom. A knowledge of Swedish, for example, was essential for education in Finland, even in the primary schools. Parents therefore tried to give their children a knowledge of the language before sending them to school; Finnish was considered the *patois* language of peasants and laborers. In an attempt to counter such beliefs, a Finnish newspaper was founded in 1821 by Adolf Iwar Arwidsson. A poet, historian and newspaperman, Arwidsson was the first man of stature in the Finnish language movement. He used his paper to prod his countrymen to a realization of the need for Finnish. He believed that language was the main criterion of a national movement, uniting those who speak a common tongue into a natural indivisible whole. In 1823, Arwidsson had to flee to Sweden as the Russians began to see how dangerous his views were.

After a lull, Finnish nationalism developed again very rapidly during the 1840s. During this time, the language movement began to make an impression on authorities, and provision was made at the university for theology students to learn Finnish. In 1850, the first Finnish professorship was established, and in 1851, civil servants were told that promotions in Finnish speaking areas depended on their knowledge of Finnish. By 1858, the language was introduced into the administration. Translators were provided to the provincial governments; Finnish was declared the official language of the proceedings of the church and county assemblies; and, though Swedish remained the official language of the country, Finnish was declared to have complete equality in all matters. However, because of opposition from the Swedish speaking Finns, the government dragged its feet on Finnish-Swedish equality and it was not until 1902 that the Finnish language finally gained full and equal recognition with Swedish.

In the long run, it was because of nationalism and through education that the Finnish patriots won the battle. From the beginning, they had set out to inspire Finns to be proud of their language and to be sure of their national identity. Starting with the primary schools, the reading of history and the singing of folk songs, they established positive attitudes in the children. Slowly the language spread to secondary schools, then to universities. The use of the language was a force strong enough to weld a nation state out of what had been accepted for centuries as just another region of Sweden. In 1919, the Finnish Socialists used the Russian Revolution to declare a Finnish state. However, this led to a bitter civil war between the socialists and the bourgeoisie. An independent Finland emerged with Finnish as its national language. Although Swedish was made the second official language with guaranteed rights of use, more and more young people chose to identify themselves as Finnish speakers.

The Finnish case illustrates the defining characteristics of language revitalization. First, unlike revival, there must be native speakers. The language is used as a normal means of communication and does go through the normal processes of change. In addition, revitalization is marked by the imparting of new vigor to the language through the expansion of its domains and frequently of increased institutional power to its speakers. With Finnish, for example, language use spread to include the legal proceedings of the courts of law, public administration, and medium of instruction in the schools. As mentioned earlier, Korean spread through the domain of mass media. The expansion of domains is usually preceded by some sort of status planning legislation and/or corpus planning, if the language has not been standardized or modernized. The result of this is that literacy and education become crucial factors in the mechanism for revitalization.

The obvious question then is: what conditions are necessary for revitalization to take place? From Finnish, and the other briefly mentioned case studies, we can see that nationalism is an important feature. Often following a colonial period, or even being a contributing factor to the end of colonial rule, revitalization reflects the firm and solid desire for independence and political freedom from a superstrate power. In Finland, we saw the desire for separateness from Sweden. In Tanzania, Swahili became the symbol for freedom from British colonial rule and a return to a proud African heritage. While economic advantage seems a minor factor in revitalization, the desires for independent territory and self-rule are major elements.

Another way of understanding the conditions is to examine the case of Irish, an example of language revitalization that is unsuccessful. Irish does have a small population of native speakers and the government is trying to expand its domains, by instituting mandatory language instruction in the schools, publication of Irish newspapers, and bilingual official and legal documents. However, language revitalization is not taking place because the conditions are not being met. That is, the Irish have no need to maintain a special language to produce national unity: they already have independence and territory. Additionally, the economic advantage lies primarily with English. Therefore, while there is an official movement within the government to revitalize the language, it seems destined to stop at honorary and symbolic recognition of Irish. This case, along with the successful ones, provides us with some examples of the criteria and conditions under which revitalization can occur.

Language Reversal

Distinct from revival and revitalization, language reversal implies the turning around of existing trends in the usage of a particular language. Unlike revitalization, reversal does not focus on the process of expansion of domains (although expansion may be a result); rather, it focuses on circumstances where one of the languages of a state begins to move back into more prominent use. Therefore, it is the relationship of one language within a state vis-à-vis another which marks reversal. The criteria and conditions for this situation distinguish not only reversal from revitalization, but also different kinds of reversal. That is, under the label of language reversal, we can distinguish three types: legal reversal, reversal of shift and rebound of an exoglossic language.

As previously mentioned, during the late 19th century, Catalan went through a period of revitalization, which included extensive corpus planning (such as spelling reforms). Later, during the Franco period, Catalan was illegal. However, a strong sense of nationalism kept the language not only alive but vibrant. Masses were conducted in Catalan and its very use became a political statement (Paulston, 1987a). In addition, since Catalunya had been the economic center of Spain since the 1800s, the economic advantage of that area supported the sense of nationalism and power of her people. Following the death of Franco in 1975, a *legal reversal* took place: beginning with the new constitution of Spain in 1978, Catalan was granted the opportunity to attain official status within its autonomous region along with the national and official Castilian Spanish (Siguan, 1988:452); this status was achieved in 1984. With Catalan, we have a situation where the language was in use, but technically illegal. The shift in political power resulted in legal acceptance, and economic advantage, past and present, furthered this acceptance into an expansion of domains.

The second type of reversal is *reversal of shift*. Unlike legal reversal, reversal of shift refers to a situation where a language, which appears to be disappearing, has a renascence and is saved from extinction by increased use. *Te reo Maori*, the language of the Maori people of New Zealand, is at present claimed to be undergoing a reversal of shift which many people hope will result in its preservation and growth. Archaeological evidence indicates that the Maori people landed in New Zealand as early as 900 CE; they were a village-dwelling society numbering about 250,000 when James Cook arrived in 1769. With the British occupation, their land and numbers decreased, and now, Maoris make up about 10% of the total population of New Zealand. While there has always existed a generation of Maori speakers, fewer and fewer young people learn the language. Since economic opportunities existed only outside their communities, many left for urban areas; this resulted in an increase in exogamy, and the danger of the language dying became great. However, during the late 1960s, many Maori people, proud of their special identity, began to show a growing concern with issues of land rights, political equality and the native language. In 1967, the Maori people were allowed political representation in parliament for the first time and integration within the school system. In 1986, New Zealand recognized Maori as an indigenous and official language of the country. In order to foster a sense of equality and respect for minorities and other cultures, the Department of Education has deemed it important for all students to learn about Maori culture in social studies classes (Benton, 1988). Additionally, *Language Nests* were established in 1981. Immersion programs have been set up in many primary schools and, beyond primary schools, students can take optional Maori language classes where offered. Many believe that real progress is being made and that the language is being used by more and more people in an exciting process of reversal of shift (Spolsky, 1989). However, others, such as Shafer (1988), appear less optimistic about the results, claiming that the educational system and the status planning reforms of the government only foster goals of cultural preservation and segregation. Additionally, discrimination still seems prevalent, and many young Maori must still migrate to the cities in order to find work, where the advantage in maintaining their language does not exist. The exogamy already mentioned increases with migration and lowers the chances for the language to survive. Whether the reversal of shift from a dying to a more commonly used *Te reo Maori* will be successful is still in question.

The final type of reversal involves an adopted language not indigenous to the state. As we have seen with Tanzania, for example, while the government chose to adopt Swahili after independence, higher education and commerce are still conducted in English. In order to develop and compete economically in a world market, the *rebound of an exoglossic language* sometimes occurs. Singapore provides us with an excellent case study of this phenomenon.

The Republic of Singapore consists of the main island of Singapore and some sixty islets within its territorial waters. The total land area is only 226 square miles, but within this compact country thrives a multi-ethnic and multilingual community. Officially, Singapore's population of 2.6 million has the following components: 77% Chinese, 15% Malay, 6% Indian, and 2% other, which includes Eurasians, Europeans, and Arabs (Sudderuddin, 1985:29). Such heterogeneity, in terms of ethnic identification, does not reflect the actual complexities of the linguistic situation in Singapore, since each of the three major ethnic groups (Chinese, Malay, Indian) also retain a variety of languages and/or dialects as subgroups. For example, the ethnic Chinese speak natively one or more of the following dialects, linguistically classified as languages: Hokkien, Teochew, Cantonese, Mandarin, Hakka, Foochow, Hainese, and other less familiar dialects.

Language questions have been of great importance in Singapore since its founding as an English settlement in 1817. With no dominant culture which immigrants could adopt or be forced to assimilate to, each of the arriving groups maintained its homeland culture to a high degree, many feeling that they were transitory in the country. The basic language policy decisions which have had an important effect in Singapore are those affecting the education system, the civil service and other official areas. Until 1920, education was available in English, Chinese dialects, Malay and sporadically in Tamil. With the change in policy towards language in mainland China, Mandarin was introduced to all Chinese schools in the 1920s.

Malays had access to primary education solely in the Malay language and only a few could then advance to secondary education, which was in English. Several types of educational systems functioned side-by-side divided not only by who financed them (e.g. government, missionary societies, ethnic communities), but also by the type of education being given (e.g. religious, political, general). This produced a dividing line by the type of education one had received: English-educated, Chinese-educated or Indian-educated. The sharpest division was found between the English- and Chinese-educated in the ethnic Chinese community. The Chinese-educated continued with the traditional pattern of education found in mainland China, whereas the English-educated learned not only English but also the culture and tradition of the western world. English was associated with economic and educational rewards; it was the language of the colonial government, the legal system and of that part of the business world which was directed towards the west.

After independence in 1965, the prestige associated with English remained, although the new government, formed by the People's Action Party, began a policy of equal treatment for the four main ethnic groups and their languages. The linguistically diverse situation in Singapore has been tempered by a policy of bilingual education introduced in 1956 as a result of the All-Party report which recommended that the four languages designated as official — English, Chinese (Mandarin), Malay and Tamil — be available as media of instruction (Gopinathan, 1980:181). Bilingual education in Singapore's schools has been the policy since then, but not without several modifications in successive stages, which have given increasing emphasis to English. Today, there is no longer the choice of main medium of education — English is the language of instruction in all schools, with another official language as secondary in almost all cases. "Bilingualism" in Singapore has come to be defined as "proficiency in English and one other official language" (Tay, 1983:176).

Thus, although Singapore has four official languages, English is by far the most important to know. It is the language of survival, crucial to the development and maintenance of all the economic sectors making up the nation's livelihood on the one hand, and to the maintenance of communication and information with the international and regional community, on the other. English is the language of government, of trade, and of education. The de facto working language for the greater part of the population, it has also assumed increasing importance at home with the present generation of Singaporeans.

Language reversal, then, refers to internal situations within a state where some course changes direction. With legal reversal, we have the legal recognition of a language which is already in use. Thus Catalan changed from an illegal to a legal language following the death of Franco and his repressive language policies. Reversal of shift refers to the action of individuals belonging to linguistic minorities within a state who move to increase the use of their common language. Fishman (1990) suggests that this can be done only by starting at the family level, then moving to the neighborhood or community level, then, finally, to a larger level. Considering the Language Nests and other status planning objectives of the New Zealand government, this seems to be the attempt with the Maori language. Finally, rebound of an exoglossic language requires a specific set of circumstances in which a language, not native to the state, becomes re-accepted after a period of rejection and is used primarily for economic advantage and communication with the world community.

Conclusion

Our attempt here has been to establish a clear terminology for the discussion of various linguistic situations which have not had generally accepted definitions. Under the general category of language regenesis, the case studies discussed here share some basic characteristics. They all involve the description and explanation of group behavior relating to the increased use of dead, dying or neglected languages. In a general sense, then, they fall into the same category, which we have labeled language regenesis. In a more specific sense, language regenesis can be subcategorized into distinct subfields — language revival, revitalization and reversal. Among these subfields, case studies can illustrate the differences and one can see, for example, that the revival of Hebrew is not a parallel situation to the legal recognition of Catalan or the expanded use of Finnish. Revival refers to a specific set of criteria and conditions whereby a dead language becomes, not only revived, but the normal means of communication within a speech community. Revitalization refers to situations where a subordinate language experiences new energy and strength through expanded use. Finally, reversal encompasses several different situations: the legal acknowledgment of a language, the shift and increase in usage of a language, or the rebound of a language not indigenous to the state. While these categories share similarities, the particular situations under which they occur reveal specific differences in objectives, mobilization and implementation.

Additionally, it needs to be pointed out that these categories are not exclusive. That is, at different points in its development, a language may experience different phases. For example, after the revival, Hebrew went through a period of revitalization where the language modernized and expanded its domains. Finnish went through a long period of revitalization, after which it received the legal recognition of the government. Unlike Catalan, Finnish was never illegal, but it had not been recognized as an official language. Moreover, these movements are not always successful, as we have seen with Irish, and the success of the reversal of Maori is still in question.

Chapter 8

Epilogue

I already knew when I began this work that the major influence on the results of bilingual education was whether it took place in a situation of language maintenance or language shift (as well as factors concomitant to maintenance and shift, such as social status whether economic, religious, ascribed etc.)

What I did not know were the social determinants of maintenance or shift or how to predict these phenomena. I was concerned because I was occasionally asked officially (Chapter 3, e.g. was originally written as a report to OECD, Paris) for analysis, recommendations and evaluation of educational language policies for minorities. So, for example, in my report to the Swedish National Board of Education (1982), I was able to point out that while mother tongue education for the immigrant children was a positive experience for most of them (for some it served as a means of segregation), strictly speaking it was not necessary since the situation in which it took place was one of very rapid shift to Swedish. What was more important was a good program in Swedish as a Second Language which was practically nonexistent. Of course such recommendations were highly controversial and denounced by some for primarily ideological reasons. It would have been useful at the time to have had a theoretical model on which to legitimate the recommendations.

Motivated by my Catalan and Swedish fieldwork, I set to work to explain the course of mother tongue diversity in nations, to use Lieberson's phrasing. Just why was Catalan maintained but not Occitan? Basically this comparative approach was the same I followed throughout in a comparison of case studies.

As always when you want to learn something, one of the best ways to find out is to teach a course in it. For three enjoyable years, I taught a course on "Language in Ethnicity and Nationalism," once I had begun to develop the model, where each student chose a case study and did their level best to test the theoretical frame work, which indeed was modified several times due to the inability to deal with some of their data. We always went back to facts in testing the model.

The final form of the model is sketched out in the chart on page 110.

I see the social determinants, i.e. the independent variables, the causal factors, of language maintenance and shift as four different types of social mobilization, namely ethnicity, ethnic movement, ethnic nationalism and geographic nationalism. Below their headings are listed those social features which serve as the defining characteristics of each movement and which are discussed at length in chapter 3.

But the result of the social mobilization will not always be the same; ethnicity frequently results in shift but not always. Next we need to consider what may be thought of as intervening or contextual variables. Do the dominant and subordinate group agree or disagree on collective goals for the latter (Schermerhorn, see page 18)? If there is agreement on assimilation, are there incentives to bring it about? The proposition "Jobs select language learning strategies" (Brudner, 1972) is very powerful in accounting for data, but this is one area where we should be able to further extend our knowledge and explanations.

And finally we have the dependent variables, that which is to be explained, the results of the social mobilization in language maintenance or shift. With rapid shift, agreement on goals, access to the language and incentives in the form of jobs, there is very little need for complicated educational policies. With slow shift, as on the Navajo reservation, bilingual education becomes much more important, if not crucial, for participation in the life of the nation.

Ethnic nationalism will tend to maintain its language, as Catalunya has done, or bring about a revitalization as was the case with Finland. Language policies here involve considerable corpus planning, as we have seen with Hebrew, Finnish and Korean. In many cases, status planning also was involved, not always before corpus planning as is the general wisdom.

Geographic nationalism is similar to ethnic nationalism in maintenance of the national language, but may have more than one national language. There is usually the same importance placed on literacy in the standardized and modernized language. Whether nation-states based on ethnic nationalism, like Finland and Turkey, treat their minorities with more or less tolerance than do states based on geographic nationalism, like Canada and Nigeria (an arguable example) is a question which remains unexamined. I would probably argue that the answer lies with the contextual variables and follow Schermerhorn's argument. But that is a question which deserves more study.

I have spoken about linguistic implications of social mobilization, but the next step that needs to be worked out in detail is a typology of educational models in multilingual settings, where language maintenance and shift are considered as intervening variables. We need to be able to consider optimum programs in a range of possibilities and to do so in an informed fashion.

Table 1. Linguistic consequences of social mobilization in multilingual settings

	Ethnicity	Ethnic Movement	Ethnic Nationalism	Geographic Nationalism
(1) Defining characteristics	As identity	As strategy in competion for scarce resources	Territory	
	Unconscious learned behaviour		Closed nationalism (Kohn) exclusive	Open nationalism
		Goal: socioeconomic advantage		
	Shared ancestors; roots		Intellectual leaders Middle class Loyalty (important)	
	Taken for granted Not goal oriented No violence	Cognitive Self-chosen Militant Violent	Common enemy Taught behaviours	
	Common values and beliefs	Charismatic leader Language as rallying point Boundary maintenance	Goal: independence, political self-determination	
	Survives language shift	Glorious Past	External distinction Internal cohesion (Haugen)	
		Cultural self-determination		
			as identity	
	Less <─────── Legislation Involved ───────> More			
(2) Facilitating or constraining factors	? Under what social conditions? E.g. Participation in social institutions, schooling, exogamy, military service, religious institutions; mass-media; roads and transportation; travel, trade, commerce, war, evangelism; occupations; in-migration, back-migration, urbanization, etc.			
(3) Linguistic consequences	Language shift	Language shift but slower rate	Maintenance national language as powerful symbol	Maintenance national language
Also: Language spread Language death Language reformation			Language planning academies	
			Strong language attitudes	
			Standardization Modernization Literacy-teacher training Language problems: Choice of national language	

Notes

1. I am following the terminology of common practice in using the term minority but want to point out that in dealing with language outcomes, subordinate status is almost always more important than mere numbers.

2. Most studies on bilingual education are done from a psychological perspective with the individual as the unit of research. I am here solely interested in the language behavior of *groups*.

3. By group bilingualism I mean a group where all or most of the individual members are bilingual. This is not necessarily true of countries who legally recognize more than one national language. For example, German speaking Swiss do not typically speak French and Italian as well.

4. I should make clear that Rodriguez is criticized for ideological reasons by proponents for bilingual education, not for the quality of his writing.

5. Dell Hymes has coined the term communicative competence (1972) to include not only the linguistic forms of a language but also a knowledge of when, how and to whom it is appropriate to use these forms. Communicative competence includes the social meaning of the linguistic forms, and Hymes points out that were a man to stand on a street corner and utter all and only the grammatical sentences of English (Chomsky's definition of linguistic competence), he likely would be institutionalized.

6. In the preceding paragraph he talks about the "invidious connotations of tribalism". Whatever those connotations are, social scientists have "scrapped" the term *tribe* altogether, which for my purposes I regret since there is no more accurate way to discuss language problems and social organization in e.g. Somalia and Kurdistan.

7. Although it would be misleading to claim that structural-functional theory has given way to neo-marxism. The leading research paradigm on e.g. bilingual education remains a structural-functional perspective (albeit with notable exceptions [see Paulston 1980, 1982]) which at times leads to infelicitous claims because the very nature of ethnic groups in contact frequently tends towards conflict, and so group conflict theory may hold greater insight. On the other hand, in situations marked by calm and basic good will, neo-marxist theory can lead to misleading interpretations and mischief-making claims.

8. I am here only talking from a viewpoint of educational efficiency. There are many other strong arguments for mother tongue teaching of an affective nature (Gaarder, 1977; Pascual, 1976; Pialorsi, 1974; Sevilla-Casas et al., 1973). There is also the argument that languages are national resources which are being wasted without support in the educational systems (Fishman, 1972b).

9. That life may be after death, as in Jihad, Holy War.

10. All linguists know that we owe the original impetus for our discipline to Pāṇini who more than two thousand years ago devised a way of describing the sound system of Sanskrit to keep people from changing the pronunciation.

11. The significance of symbols can change. During the Vietnamese war, to fly the flag in the United States meant that you supported the war, and flag-burning was common. During this time, the U.S. flag lost a great deal of its *national* symbolism, but this significance has been restored as was obvious during the Olympic games in Los Angeles.

12. In psychology, "Intervening variable is a term invented to account for internal and directly unobservable psychological processes that in turn account for behavior..." (Kerlinger, 1973:40). This is different from its use in the social sciences where intervening or contextual variables "modify the effects of independent variables" (Schermerhorn, 1970:15). In this sense contextual variables help account for the conditions for and the modes of integration (or lack of) of ethnic groups and are perfectly observable, like cultural congruence.

13. The spelling of "Catalonia" as "Catalunya" in English, which is not uncommon, is an affectation, but one of a positive kind. "Catalunya", the Catalan spelling, contrasts with "Cataluña" in Castilian and, when used in English, announces the writer's probias for matters Catalan.

14. There are of course incurable optimists; see for instance the Newsletter #4, April 1993 and the list of Events of Mercator-Education: European network for regional or minority languages and education, Fryske Akademy, Doelestrjitte 8, Ljouvert, The Netherlands.

15. "As a political unit it will presumably be more effective if it is also a social unit. Like any unit, it minimizes internal differences and maximizes external ones. On the individual's personal and local identity it superimposes a national one by identifying his ego with that of all others within the nation and separating it from that of all others outside the nation. In a society that is essentially familial or tribal or regional it stimulates a loyalty beyond the primary groups, but discourages any conflicting loyalty to other nations. The ideal is: internal cohesion-external distinction" (Haugen 1972: 244).

16. In this discussion, I am excluding a consideration of the Finns and the Sami (Lapps) in the very north of Sweden, who came into contact with the Swedes through annexation. Certainly the reindeer-herding Sami have a very different culture from the Swedes nor are they really thought of as Swedes. In any case,

the Swedish Finns and Sami are undergoing massive language shift (Johansson, 1977; Rönmark and Wikström, 1980) in spite of occasional counterclaims.

17. From Hungary in the 1950s and Czechoslovakia, Poland in the 1960s and later from Latin America especially Chile, Turkey, Vietnam, Uganda, Iran, Poland, and Lebanon.

18. Care is needed in the comparison with national norms. Such statistics are normed on children from all social classes, and since social class correlates positively with school achievement, Finnish working class children in Finland will also be below the norms.

19. Of Steen's (1980) children, 67% claimed to be dominant in Swedish.

20. Presumably the gymnasium statistics indicate that the immigrant children show higher upward social mobility than do the Swedish children since the figures of Swedish children include all social classes while the immigrant children are mostly working class.

21. 1958, A commission of the Restoration of the Irish Language; 1965, 1966, 1969 White Paper; 1975, Committee on Language Attitude Research; 1978 Bord na Gaeilge; 1980 White Paper (Edwards, 1984:272).

22. The Gaeltacht in western Ireland is the only area which still retains a "critical mass" of native speakers of Irish. Edwards estimates that there may be 50,000 regular Irish speakers left (1984:271). The maintenance of Irish in the Gaeltacht is obviously crucial to the survival of Irish as a living language.

23. A network model of bilingualism differs from a domain model in that both languages can be used in all domains and are equally appropriate. Rather, it is one's "network" of individual friends and acquaintances who determines language choice, a function of two languages in contact which is not conducive to language maintenance.

24. Bernard Spolsky finds the term reversal to be negative (personal communication, March 1992). We intend no such connotation and refer simply to a change in present legislation, i.e. legal reversal, in order to more accurately reflect existing ideology and linguistic trends.

"Restoration by law" may at first seem a preferable term, but it is misleading in many cases; sometimes there is nothing to restore, because it never existed before or because it always existed. E. g. Faroese never needed any restoration, just a recognition by law of its existence. Driven by growing nationalist consciousness, the Faroese finally in 1948 were able to change, to reverse Danish law to include Faroese as principal, official language. But there never was a question of restoration.

We would like here to acknowledge Bernard Spolsky's helpful comments on this chapter.

25. Bernard Spolsky disagrees with this point while R. L. Cooper does not. See Spolsky and Cooper, 1991.

Bibliography

Abd al-Latif Sharara, 1962. "The Idea of Nationalism". In Sylvia Haim (ed.), *Arab Nationalism*. Berkeley.
Abdulaziz, M. H. 1982. "Patterns of Language Acquisition and Use in Kenya: Rural-Urban Differences", *International Journal of the Sociology of Language* 34: 95-120.
Abel, F. 1973. *Le mouvement occitaniste contemporain dans la région de Toulouse, d'après les articles occitans parus dans la "Dépêche du Midi" (1969-1972)*. Tübingen: Gunter Narr.
Akzin, Benjamin. 1964. *State and Nation*. London: Hutchinson.
Alba, Victor. 1975. *Catalonia: A Profile*. New York: Praeger.
Albert, M. and L. Obler. 1978. *The Bilingual Brain*. New York: Academic Press.
Albo, Xavier. 1970. "Social Constraints on Cochabamba Quechua". Latin American Studies Program, Dissertation Series. Ithaca, NY: Cornell University.
Anderson, E., Faria, F., Olsson, J. 1980. *Hemspråk i förskola och skola i Lunds kommun*. Lund: Local School Board.
Aracil, L. 1983. *Dir la realitat*. Barcelona: Ed. Paisos Catalans.
Asmah Haji Omar. 1979. *Language Planning for Unity and Efficiency*. Kuala Lumpur: Penerbit Universiti Malaya.
Azevedo, M. M. 1984. "The Re-establishment of Catalan as a Language of Culture", *Hispanic Linguistics* 1(2): 305-330.
Badia i Margarit, A. M. 1969. *La llengua dels barcelonins: resultats d'una enquesta sociologico-linguistica*, Vol. 1. Barcelona: Edicions 62.
Badia i Margarit, A. M. 1972. *Llengua i cultura als paisos catalans*. Barcelona: Edicions 62.
Baetens Beardsmore, H. 1993. *European Models of Bilingual Education*. Clevedon: Multilingual Matters
Baker, C. 1993. *Foundations of Bilingual Education and Bilingualism*. Clevedon: Multilingual Matters.
Barth, F. 1969. *Ethnic Groups and Boundaries*. Boston, MA: Little Brown & Co.
Bauman, J. J. 1980. *A Guide to Issues in Indian Language Retention*. Washington, DC: Center for Applied Linguistics.
Bec, P. 1967. *La langue occitane*. Paris: Presses Universitaires de France.

Bennett, John W. 1975a. "A Guide to the Collection". In J. Bennett (ed.), *The New Ethnicity: Perspectives from Ethnology*. St. Paul: West Publishing.
Bennett, John W. 1975b. *The New Ethnicity: Perspectives from Ethnology*. St. Paul: West Publishing.
Benton, Richard A. 1988. "The Maori Language in New Zealand Education", *Language, Culture and Curriculum* 1 (2): 75-83.
Bokamba, E.D. 1981. "Language and National Development in Sub-Saharan Africa: a Progress Report", *Studies in the Linguistic Sciences* 11: 1-25.
Bord na Gaeilge. 1988. *The Irish Language in a Changing Society: Shaping the Future*. Dublin: Bord na Gaeilge.
Bord na Gaeilge. 1989. *Key to the Irish Language*. Dublin: Bord na Gaeilge.
Boyd, S. 1984. "Minoritets språken är borta om 25 år?", *Invandrare och Minoriteter*, 5/6:43-45.
Breton. R. J.-L. 1991. *Geolinguistics: Language Dynamics and Ethnolinguistic Geography*. Ottawa: Ottawa University Press.
Brochetti, C. 1992. "In Defense of our Common Tongue. The Official English Movement: Language Planning and Policy in the U.S." Pittsburgh, PA. MS.
Brudner, L. 1972. "The Maintenance of Bilingualism in Southern Austria", *Ethnology* 11(1):39-54.
Brudner, L. and D. White. 1979. "Language Attitudes: Behavior and Intervening Variables". In W. F. Mackey and J. Ornstein (eds.), *Sociolinguistic Studies in Language Contact*. The Hague: Mouton.
Bryan, M. A. 1959. *The Bantu Languages of Africa*. London: Oxford University Press for International African Institute.
Candel, F. 1964. *Els Altres Catalans*. Barcelona: Edicions 62.
Carillo, L. 1984. "Reflections on Rodriguez' *Hunger of Memory*". *TESOL Newsletter*, 18(5):9-30.
Castile, G. P. and G. Kushner. 1981. *Persistent Peoples*. Tuscon: University of Arizona Press.
Cazden, C. B. and C. E. Snow (eds.) 1990. *English Plus*. Special issue: *Annals of the American Academy of Political and Social Science*.
Center for Applied Linguistics. 1977. *Bilingual Education: Current Perspectives*. 5 vol. Arlington VA.
Churchill, S. 1986. *The Education of Linguistic and Cultural Minorities in the OECD Countries*. San Diego, CA: College-Hill Press.
Cohen, A. and M. Swain. 1976. "Bilingual Education: The 'Immersion Model' in the North American Context". *TESOL Quarterly* 10(1):45-53.
Committee on Language Attitudes Research (CLAR). 1975. Report. Dublin: Stationery Office.
Cooper, R. L. 1982. "A Framework for the Study of Language Spread". *Language Spread: Studies in Diffusion and Social Change*. Arlington, VA: Center for Applied Linguistics, and Bloomington, IN: Indiana University Press.

Cooper, R. L. 1989. *Language Planning and Social Change*. Cambridge: Cambridge University Press.
Cottam, R. W. 1964. *Nationalism in Iran*. Pittsburgh: University of Pittsburgh Press.
Council of Europe. 1976. *Factors which Influence the Integration of Migrants' Children into Pre-school Education in France*. Strasbourg: Council for Cultural Cooperation.
Crawford, J. 1992. *Language Loyalties: A Source Book on the Official English Controversy*. Chicago: University of Chicago Press.
Crewe, W. (ed.) 1977. *The English Language in Singapore*. Singapore: Eastern Universities Press.
Cummins, J. 1976. "The Influence of Bilingualism on Cognitive Growth: A Synthesis of Research Findings and Explanatory Hypothesis", *Working Papers on Bilingualism* 9:1-43.
Cummins, J. 1988a. Review of "Language Planning in Ireland", *International Journal of the Sociology of Language* 70:303-308.
Cummins, J. 1988b. "Foreword". *Aspects of Bilingual Education: The Italian and Irish Experience*. Dublin: Bord na Gaeilge.
Cummins, J. and M. Swain. 1986. *Bilingualism in Education*. London: Longman.
Dakota Indian Foundation Newsletter. March, 1985. Chamberlain, South Dakota.
de Vries, J. 1977. "Explorations in the Demography of Language: Estimation of Net Language Shift in Finland 1961-1970", *Acta Sociologica* 20(2):145-153.
Deutsch, K. W. 1953. *Nationalism and Social Communication: An Inquiry into the Foundations of Nationality*. Cambridge, MA: MIT Press.
DeVos, G. and L. Romanucci-Ross. 1975. "Ethnicity: Vessel of Meaning and Emblem of Contrast". In *Ethnic Identity: Cultural Continuities and Change*. Palo Alto: Mayfield.
Días López, C. 1980. "Diglossia and Social Cleavage: The Case of Galicia". In P. Nelde (ed.), *SprachKontakt und SprachKonflikt*. Wiesbaden: F. Steiner.
Dorian, N. 1981. *Language Death: The Life Cycle of a Scottish Gaelic Dialect*. Philadelphia: University of Pennsylvania Press.
Dorian, N. 1987. "The Value of Language-maintenance Efforts which are Unlikely to Succeed", *International Journal of the Sociology of Language* 68:57-67.
Douhan, B. 1982. "The Walloons in Sweden", *American-Swedish Genealogical Review* 2:1-17.
Dressler, W. and R. Wodak-Leodolter (eds.). 1977. *Language Death*. Special Issue: *International Journal of the Sociology of Language*, 12.
Eckert, P. 1980. "Diglossia: Separate and Unequal", *Linguistics* 18:1053-1064.
Eckert, P. 1983. "The Paradox of National Language Movements", *Journal of Multilingual and Multicultural Development* 4(4): 289-300.

Edwards, J. (ed.) 1984. *Linguistic Minorities, Policies and Pluralism*. London: Academic Press.
Edwards, J. 1985. *Language, Society and Identity*. Oxford: Blackwell.
Ekstrand, L. H. 1981. "Språk, Identitet, Kultur." *Reprints and Miniprints, 391*. Malmö: School of Education.
Ekvall, U. 1979. *Ordval i skriftlig framställning hos 'invandrarelever' och svenska elever*. University of Stockholm.
Elazar, D., and M. Friedman. 1976. *Moving Up: Ethnic Succession in America*. New York: Institute on Pluralism and Group Identity of the American Jewish Committee.
Ellis, P. B. and Seumas mac a'Ghobhainn. 1971. *The Problem of Language Revival*. Inverness: Club Leabhar.
Emerson, Rupert. 1960. *From Empire to Nation: The Rise to Self-Assertion of Asian and African Peoples*. Cambridge, MA: Harvard University Press.
Engle, P.L. 1975. *The Use of Vernacular Languages in Education: Language Medium in Early School Years for Minority Language Groups*. Arlington, VA: Center for Applied Linguistics.
Escobar, A. (ed.) 1972. *El reto del multilinguismo en el Perú*. Perú-Problema No. 9. Lima: Instituto de Estudios Peruanos.
Escobar, A. 1988. "Bilingualism in Peru". In C. B. Paulston (ed.), *International Handbook of Bilingualism and Bilingual Education*. New York: Greenwood Press.
Fase, W., K. Jaspaert, and S. Kroon. 1992. *Maintenance and Loss of Minority Languages*. Amsterdam: John Benjamins.
Fasold, R. 1984. *The Sociolinguistics of Society*. Oxford:Blackwell.
Ferguson, C. 1959. "Diglossia", *Word* 15:325-340.
Ferguson, C. 1971. *Language Structure and Language Use*. Stanford: Stanford University Press.
Ferguson, C. 1991. "Diglossia revisited", *Southwest Journal of Linguistics*. 10(1): 214-234.
Fishman, J. A. 1964. "Language Maintenance and Language Shift as a Field of Inquiry", *Linguistics* 9:32-70.
Fishman, J. A. 1966. *Language Loyalty in the United States*. The Hague: Mouton.
Fishman, J. A. 1968. "Nationality-Nationalism and Nation-Nationism." In J.A. Fishman, C. Ferguson, & J. DaGupta (eds.), *Language Problems in Developing Nations*. New York: Wiley.
Fishman, J. A. 1971. "The Sociology of Language: An Interdisciplinary Social Science Approach to Language in Society". In J.A. Fishman (ed.), *Advances in the Sociology of Language*, Vol. 1. The Hague: Mouton.
Fishman, J. A. 1972a. *Advances in the Sociology of Language*, Vol. 2. The Hague: Mouton.

Fishman, J.A. 1972b. *Language in Sociocultural Change*. Stanford, CA: Stanford University Pres.
Fishman, J. A. 1972c. *Language and Nationalism: Two Integrative Essays*. Rowley, MA: Newbury House.
Fishman, J. A. 1973. "Language Modernization and Planning in Comparison with other Types of National Modernization and Planning", *Language in Society* 2(1):23-42.
Fishman, J. A. 1977a. "The Spread of English as a New Perspective for the Study of Language Shift". In J. A. Fishman, R. L. Cooper and A. W. Conrad (eds.), *The Spread of English: The Sociology of English as Additional Language*. Rowley, MA: Newbury House.
Fishman, J. A. 1977b. "Language Maintenance", *Harvard Encyclopedia of American Ethnic Groups*. Cambridge University Press.
Fishman, J. A. 1990. "What is Reversing Language Shift (RLS) and How Can It Succeed?", *Journal of Multilingual and Multicultural Development* 11(1 & 2):5-36.
Fishman, J., C. Ferguson and J. DaGupta (eds.), 1968. *Language Problems in Developing Nations*. New York: Wiley.
J. A. Fishman, R. L. Cooper and A. W. Conrad (eds.), 1977. *The Spread of English: The Sociology of English as Additional Language*. Rowley, MA: Newbury House.
Gaarder, B. 1977. "Language Maintenance or Language Shift". In W. F. Mackey & T. Anderson (eds.), *Bilingualism in Early Childhood*. Rowley, MA: Newbury House.
Gal, S. 1979. *Language Shift: Social Determinants of Linguistic Change in Bilingual Austria*. New York: Academic Press.
Garcia, O. (ed.) 1991. *Bilingual Education*. Amsterdam: John Benjamins.
Gendron, J. D. 1972. *The Position of the French Language in Quebec*. Quebec: L'editeur officiel de Quebec.
Giner, S. 1980. *The Social Structure of Catalonia*. University of Sheffield: Anglo-Catalan Society.
Glazer, N. 1966. "The Process and Problems of Language Maintenance: An Integrative Review. In J.A. Fishman (ed.), *Language Loyalty in the United States*. The Hague: Mouton.
Glazer, N. 1983. *Ethnic Dilemmas*. Cambridge, MA: Harvard University Press.
Glazer, N. and D. P. Moynihan. 1975 "Introduction". In *Ethnicity: Theory and Experience*. Cambridge: Harvard University Press,
Glinert, L. 1991. "The 'Back to the Future' Syndrome in Language Planning: The Case of Modern Hebrew". In D. Marshall (ed.), *Language Planning*. Amsterdam: John Benjamins.
Gopinathan, S. 1980. "Language Policy in Education: A Singapore Perspective". In E.A. Afendras and E.C.Y. Kuo (eds.), *Patterns of Bilingualism*. Singapore: RELC Anthology Series, Number 8.

Gordon, D. C. 1978. *The French Language and National Identity (1930-1975)*. The Hague: Mouton.
Grandguillaume, G. 1983. *Arabisation et politique linguistique au Maghreb*. Paris: Maisonneuve & Larose.
Grimshaw, A. D. 1971. "Sociolinguistics." In J.A. Fishman (ed.), *Advances in the Sociology of Language*, Vol. 1. The Hague: Mouton.
Grosjean, F. 1982. *Life with Two Languages: An Introduction to Bilingualism*. Cambridge, MA: Harvard University Press.
Hamers, J. F. and M. H. A. Blanc. 1989. *Bilinguality and Bilingualism*. Cambridge: Cambridge University Press.
Hansegård, N. E. 1968. *Tvåspråkighet eller halvspråkighet?* Stockholm: Aldus/Bonniers
Harris, J. and L. Murtagh. 1987. "Irish and English in Gaeltacht Primary Schools". In G. MacEoin, A. Ahlqvist and D. O'Haodha (eds.), *Third International Conference on Minority Languages: Celtic Papers*. Clevedon: Multilingual Matters.
Harris, J. and L. Murtagh. 1988. "National Assessment of Irish-Language Speaking and Listening Skills in Primary-school Children: Research Issues in the Evaluation of School Based Heritage-Language Programs", *Language, Culture and Curriculum* 1(2): 85-130.
Hartford, B., A. Valdman, and C. R. Foster. 1982. *Issues in International Bilingual Education*. New York: Plenum Press.
Haugen, E. 1966. "Dialect, Language, Nation", *American Anthropologist* 68(4): 922-935.
Haugen, E. 1972. *The Ecology of Language*. Stanford, CA: Stanford University Press.
Haugen, E., J. D. McClure and D. Thomson (eds.) 1990. *Minority Languages Today*. Edinburgh: University Press.
Heath, S. B. and R. Laprade. 1982. "Castilian Colonization and Indigenous Languages: The Cases of Quechua and Aymara". In R. L. Cooper (ed.), *Language Spread*. Washington, D.C.: Center for Applied Linguistics and Bloomington: Indiana University Press.
Hilmerson, B., Hägglund, E., Oscarson, M., and Stamou, E. 1980. *Attityder till språk och språkinlärning*. Department of Linguistics, University of Stockholm.
Hindley, R. 1990. *The Death of the Irish Language*. London: Routledge.
Hinnebusch, T. J. 1979. "Swahili". In T. Shopen (ed.), *Languages and their Status*. Cambridge, MA: Winthrop.
Hornberger, N. 1985. "Bilingual Education and Quechua Language Maintenance in Highland Puno, Peru". Unpublished doctoral dissertation, University of Wisconsin, Madison, WI.

Hornby, P. 1977. *Bilingualism: Psychological, Social, and Educational Implications*. New York: Academic Press.
Hyltenstam, K. 1991. "Illa genomtänkt hemspråksförslag". In *Invandrare & Minoriteter*, 2.
Hyltenstam, K. and L. Arnberg. 1988. "Bilingualism and Education of Immigrant Children and Adults in Sweden". In C. B. Paulston (ed.), *International Handbook of Bilingualism and Bilingual Education*. New York: Greenwood Press.
Hyltenstam, K., and Stroud, C. 1982. "Halvspråkighet ett förbrukat slagord," *Invandrare och minoriteter* 3:10-13.
Hymes, D. 1972. "On Communicative Competence". In Pride & Holmes (eds.), *Sociolinguistics*. Harmondsworth, England: Penguin.
Invandrarexpeditionen. 1979. *Invandrarundervisningen i Stockholms skolor*. Stockholm.
Isajiw, W. 1974. "Definitions of Ethnicity", *Ethnicity* 1:111-124.
Jaspaert, K. and S. Kroon (eds.) 1991. *Ethnic Minority Languages and Education*. Amsterdam: Swets and Zeitlinger
Jelonek, W. 1975. "Norrköpings invandrarelever avslutande grundskolan 1975 mot backgrund av den allmänna invandrarpolitiken". Del 2. Ms. Linköping University.
Jernudd, B. 1973. "Language Planning as a Type of Language Treatment". In J. Rubin and R. Shuy (eds.), *Language Planning: Current Issues and Research*. Washington, DC: Georgetown University Press.
Johansson, H. 1977. *Samerna och Sameundervisningen i Sverige*. Umeå: University of Umeå.
Kabir, M. 1985. "Changing Faces of Nationalism in Bangladesh". Unpublished doctoral dissertation, University of Pittsburgh.
Kennedy, C. 1984. *Language Planning and Language Education*. London: Allen & Unwin.
Kerlinger, F. N. 1973. *Foundations of Behavioral Research*. New York: Holt, Rinehart, & Winston.
Kirsch, P. 1977. "Review of B. Schlieben-Lange, *Okzitanisch und Katalanish. Ein Beitrag zur Soziolinguistik zweier romanischen Sprachen*", *International Journal of the Sociology of Language* 12:113-114.
Kloss, H. and G.D McConnell. 1979. *Linguistics Composition of the Nations of the World: South and Central America*. Quebec: University of Laval Press.
Kloss, H. and G. D. McConnell. 1985. *Linguistic Composition of the Nations of the World: Europe and the USSR*. Quebec: University of Laval Press.
Kohn, H. 1944. *The Idea of Nationalism: A Study of its Origins and Background*. New York: Macmillan.
Kohn, H. "Nationalism", *1968 International Encyclopedia of the Social Sciences* 11:63-70. New York: Crowell, Collier and Macmillan.

Kuhn, T. S. 1970. *The Structure of Scientific Revolutions*. Chicago: University of Chicago Press.
Kuusinen, J., Lasonen, K., and Särkelä, T. 1977. *Samband mellan undervisningsspråk och finska invandrarelevers språkfärdighet och skolprestationer*. University of Jyväskylä.
Laitner, D. 1977. *Politics, Language and Thought: The Somali Experience*. Chicago: University of Chicago Press.
Lambert, W. E. 1972. *Language, Psychology, and Culture*. Stanford, CA: Stanford University Press.
Lambert, W. and R. Tucker. 1972. *Bilingual Education of Children: The St. Lambert Experiment*. Rowley, MA: Newbury House.
"Langue et Identité Nationale", 1977. *Recherches Sociologiques* 8:1.
Lasonen, K., and Toukomaa, P. 1978. *Linguistic Development and School Achievement among Finnish Immigrant Children in Mother-Tongue Medium Classes in Sweden*. University of Jyväskylä, Education.
Levy, S. B. 1975. "Shifting Patterns of Ethnic Identification among the Hassidim". In J. W. Bennett (ed.), *The New Ethnicity*. St. Paul: West Publishing.
Lieberson, S. 1970. *Language and Ethnic Relations in Canada*. New York: Wiley.
Lieberson, S. 1981. *Language Diversity and Language Contact*. Stanford: Stanford University Press.
Lieberson, S. and T. J. Curry. 1971. "Language Shift in the United States: Some Demographic Clues", *International Migration Review* 5:125-137.
Lieberson, S., G. Dalto and M. E. Johnston. 1975. "The Course of Mother Tongue Diversity in Nations", *American Journal of Sociology* 81(1) 34-61.
Liljegren, T. 1981. "Compulsory School Leavers in 1979 with Homelanguages other than Swedish." Interim report 3. National Swedish Board of Education, Stockholm.
Liljegren, T., and Ullman, L. 1982. *Elever med annat hemspråk än svenska som gick ut grundskolan 1979*. Delrapport 4. National Swedish Board of Education, Stockholm.
Loman, B. 1974. "Till frågan om tvåspråkighet och halvspråkighet." *Språk och Samhälle*, Gleerup, Lund.
Lopez, D. E. 1978. "Chicano Language Loyalty in an Urban Setting", *Sociology and Social Research* 62:267-278.
Mackey, W. 1976. *Bilinguisme et contact des langues*. Paris: Editions Klincksiek.
Mackey, W. and J. Ornstein (eds.) 1979. *Sociolinguistic Studies in Language Contact*. The Hague: Mouton.
Macnamara, J. 1971. "Successes and Failures in the Movement for the Restoration of Irish". In J. Rubin & B. Jernudd (eds.) *Can Language Be Planned?* Honolulu: University Press of Hawaii.
Mannheim, B. 1984. "Una nacion acorrolada: Southern Peruvian Quechua Language Planning and Politics in Historical Perspective", *Language in Society* 13:291-309.

Martin-Jones, M. and S. Romaine. 1987. "Semilingualism: A Half-Baked Theory of Communicative Competence". In E. Wande, J. Anward, B. Nordberg, L. Steensland, and M. Thelander (eds.), *Aspects of Multilingualism*. Proceedings from the Fourth Nordic Symposium on Bilingualism 1984. Uppsala: Uppsala University.
McConnell, G. D. 1992. *A Macro-sociolinguistic Analysis of Language Vitality*. Quebec: Université Laval.
McNair, J. 1980. "The Contribution of the Schools to the Restoration of Regional Autonomy in Spain", *Comparative Education* 16(1): 33-44.
Miracle, A. (ed.) 1983. *Bilingualism*. Athens, GA: University of Georgia Press.
Molde, B. and D. Sharpe. 1984. *Second International Conference on Minority Languages*. Special issue: *Journal of Multilingual and Multicultural Development* 5:3-4.
Morris, H. S. 1968. "Ethnic Groups", *International Encyclopedia of the Social Sciences*. New York: Crowell, Collier and Macmillan.
Nahir, M. 1984. "Language Planning Goals: A Classification", *Language Problems and Language Planning*. 8(3):294-327.
Nahir, M. 1988. "Language Planning and Language Acquisition: The 'Great Leap' in the Hebrew Revival". In C.B. Paulston (ed.), *International Handbook of Bilingualism and Bilingual Education*. New York: Greenwood Press.
National Swedish Board of Education. 1979. *Organisation och planering for hemspråkundervisning och stödundervisning i svenska*. Stockholm.
Nyståi, S. E., and Sjöberg, T. 1976. *Språktillhörighet—skolprestation*. University of Umeå: Department of Psychology.
O'Barr, W.M. 1976. "Language Use and Language Policy in Tanzania: an Overview". In W.M.L. O'Barr & J.F. O'Barr (eds.), *Language and Politics*. The Hague: Mouton.
O'Buachalla, S. 1988. *Education Policy in Twentieth Century Ireland*. Dublin: Wolfhound Press.
O'Riagain, P. (ed.) 1988. *Language Planning in Ireland*. Special issue: *International Journal of the Sociology of Language* 70.
O'Riagain, P. 1989. "Review Symposium: The Irish Language in a Changing Society". C.B. Paulston, M. Peillion, A. Verdoodt, and S. de Freine (eds.), *Language, Culture, and Curriculum* 2(2):135-152.
Öhman, S. 1981. "Halvspråkighet som kastmärke." *Att leva med mångfalden*. Stockholm: Liber.
Oksaar, E. 1980. "Tvåspråkighet i teori och praktik." *Invandrare och Minoriteter* 5/6:43-47.
Oriol, M. 1979. "Identité produite, identité instituée, identité exprimée: confusions des théories de l'identité nationale et culturelle", *Cahiers internationaux de sociologie* 6(6): 19-28.
Pascual, H. W. 1976. La educación bilingüe: retórica y realidad. *Defensa* 4/5:4-7.

Patch, R. W. 1967. "La Parada, Lima's Market. Serrano and Criollo, the Confusion of Race with Class", *AUFSR*, West Coast South America Series, 14(2):3-9.
Paulston, C.B. 1975. "Ethnic Relations and Bilingual Education: Accounting for Contradictory Data". In R. Troike and N. Modiano (eds), *Proceedings of the First Inter-American Conference on Bilingual Education*. Arlington, VA: Center for Applied Linguistics.
Paulston, C. B. 1980. *Bilingual Education: Theories and Issues*. Rowley, MA: Newbury House.
Paulston, C. B. 1982. *Swedish Research and Debate about Bilingualism*. Stockholm: National Swedish Board of Education.
Paulston, C. B. 1986. "Social Factors in Language Maintenance and Shift". In J. Fishman et al. (eds.) *The Fergusonian Impact*, Vol. 2. Berlin: Mouton de Gruyter.
Paulston, C. B. 1987a. "Linguistic Consequences of Ethnicity and Nationalism in Multilingual Settings". In *Multicultural Education*, Paris: Organization for Economic Cooperation and Development.
Paulston, C. B. 1987b. "Catalan and Occitan: Comparative Test Cases for a Theory of Language Maintenance and Shift", *International Journal of the Sociology of Language* 63:31-62.
Paulston, C. B. (ed.) 1988. *International Handbook of Bilingualism and Bilingual Education*. New York: Greenwood Press.
Paulston, C.B. 1992. *Sociolinguistic Perspectives on Bilingual Education*. Clevedon: Multilingual Matters.
Paulston, R. G. 1970. "Estratificacion social, poder y organizacion educacional: el caso peruano", *Aportes*, 16: 92-111; also in English version "Sociocultural constraints on Peruvian educational development", *Journal of Developing Areas*, 5(3): 401-15. 1971.
Paulston, R. G. 1977. "Separate Education as an Ethnic Survival Strategy: The Finlandssvenska Case", *Anthropology and Education Quarterly*, 8:3.
Petersen, B., n.d. *Invandrarelevernas studieresultat bättre än väntat i den svenska skolan*. Ms.
Pfaff, C. W. 1981. "Sociolinguistic problems of immigrants: Foreign workers and their children in Germany ", *Language in Society* 10:155-188.
Philips, S. 1970. "Acquisition of Rules for Appropriate Speech Usage" In J. Alatis (ed.) *Bilingualism and Language Contact*. 21st Annual Roundtable, Georgetown University.
Pialorsi, F. 1974. *Teaching the Bilingual*. Tucson: University of Arizona Press.
Piatt, B. 1990. *Only English*. Albuquerque: University of New Mexico Press.
Pi-Sunyer, O. 1971. "The Maintenance of Ethnic Identity in Catalonia". In *The Limits of Integration: Ethnicity and Nationalism in Modern Europe*. Department of Anthropology Research Reports, No. 9. Amherst: University of Massachusetts.

Pi-Sunyer, O. 1985. "Catalan Nationalism". In E. A. Tiryakian and R. Rogowski (eds.), *New Nationalisms of the Developed West*. Boston: Allen and Unwin.
Polomé, E. and C.P. Hill (eds.) 1980. *Language in Tanzania*. London: International African Institute and Oxford University Press.
Posner, R. 1966. *The Romance Languages*. Garden City, NY: Anchor.
Read, Jan. 1978. *The Catalans*. London: Faber & Faber.
Rice, F. A. (ed.) 1962. *Study of the Role of Second Languages in Asia, Africa, and Latin America*. Washington DC: Center for Applied Linguistics.
Rodriguez, R. 1982. *Hunger of Memory*. Boston: Godine.
Romaine, S. 1989. *Bilingualism*. Oxford: Blackwells.
Rönmark, W., and Wikström, J. 1980. *Tvåspråkighet i Tornedalen*. University of Umeå.
Rosier, P. and W. Holm. 1980. *The Rock Point Experience: A Longitudinal Study of a Navajo School Program*. Washington DC: Center for Applied Linguistics.
Rossinyol, J. 1974. *Le problème national catalan*. The Hague: Mouton.
Royal Institute of International Affairs. 1939. "Nationalism: A Report by a Study Group." London.
Royce, A. P. 1982. *Ethnic Identity: Strategies of Diversity*. Bloomington, IN: Indiana University Press.
Rubagumya, C.M. 1986. "Language Planning in the Tanzanian Educational System: Problems and Prospects", *Journal of Multilingual and Multicultural Development* 7(4): 283-300.
Rubagumya, C.M. (ed.) 1990. *Language and Education in Africa*. Avon, England: Multilingual Matters.
Rubin, J. 1968. *National Bilingualism in Paraguay*. The Hague: Mouton.
Sachs, L. 1983. *Onda Ögat eller Bakterier*. Stockholm: Liber.
Schermerhorn, R. A. 1970. *Comparative Ethnic Relations*. New York: Random House.
Schermerhorn, R. A. 1974. "Ethnicity in the Perspective of the Sociology of Knowledge", *Ethnicity* 1:1-14.
Schlieben-Lange, B. 1971. *Okzitanisch und Katalanisch: Ein Beitrag zur Soziolinguistik zweier romanischen Sprachen*. Tübingen: Gunter Narr.
Schlieben-Lange, B. 1977. "The Language Situation in Southern France", *Linguistics* 19:101-8.
Scotton, C. M. 1972. *Choosing a Lingua Franca in an African Capital*. Edmonton, Canada and Champaign, IL: Linguistic Research Associates.
Scotton, C. M. 1978. Language in East Africa: Linguistic Patterns and Political Ideologies. In J.A. Fishman (ed.), *Advances in the Study of Societal Multilingualism*. The Hague: Mouton.
Scotton, C. M. 1988. "Patterns of Bilingualism in East Africa". In C. B. Paulston, (ed.), *International Handbook of Bilingualism and Bilingual Education*. New York: Greenwood Press.

Sevilla-Casas et al. 1973. "Addenda of Chicanos and Boricuas" to Declaration of Chicago, IX International Congress of Anthropological and Ethnological Sciences, September 7.

Shabad, G. and R. Gunther. 1982. "Language, Nationalism, and Political Conflict in Spain", *Comparative Politics* 14(4): 443-477.

Shafer, B.C. 1972. *Faces of Nationalism*. New York: Harcourt, Brace, Jovanovich.

Shafer, B.C. 1976. *Nationalism: Its Nature and Interpreters*. Washington, D.C: American Historical Association

Shafer, S.M. 1988. "Bilingual/Bicultural Education for Maori Cultural Preservation in New Zealand", *Journal of Multilingual and Multicultural Development* 9(6): 487-501.

Siguan, M. 1980. "Education and Bilingualism in Catalonia", *Journal of Multilingual and Multicultural Development* 1(3): 231-242

Siguan, M. ed. 1983. *Lenguas y educación en el ámbito del estado español*. Barcelona: Ediciones de la Universidad de Barcelona.

Siguan, M. 1984. "Language and Education in Catalonia", *Prospects: Quarterly Review of Education* (Unesco) 14(1): 107-119.

Siguan, M. 1988. "Bilingual Education in Spain". In C. B. Paulston (ed.), *International Handbook of Bilingualism and Bilingual Education*. New York: Greenwood Press.

Similä, A. 1980. "Sverige sviker sina invandrarbarn", *Invandrare och Minoriteter*, 5/6:32-39.

Sithole, N. 1960. *Obed Mutezo, the Midzimu Christian Nationalist*. Nairobi.

Smith, A. D. 1979. *Nationalism in the Twentieth Century*. New York: New York University Press.

Snyder, L. L. 1976. *Varieties of Nationalism: A Comparative Study*. Hinsdale, IL: Dryden Press.

Spicer, E. H. 1980. *The Yaquis: A Cultural History*. Tucson: University of Arizona Press.

Spolsky, B. (ed.) 1972. *The Language Education of Minority Children*. Rowley, MA: Newbury House.

Spolsky, B. 1977. "American Indian Bilingual Education", *International Journal of the Sociology of Language* 14: 57-72

Spolsky, B. 1989. "Maori Bilingual Education and Language Revitalization", *Journal of Multilingual and Multicultural Development* 10(2): 89-106.

Spolsky, B. and R. Cooper. 1991. *The Languages of Jerusalem*. Oxford: Clarendon Press.

Steen, I. 1980. *Finska invandrarungdomar i Finspång och Västerås*. Swedish State's Youth Council.

Stolt, B. 1975. "Om 'halvspråkighet' och 'språkets känslofunktion'", *Nordisk Minoritetsforsking* 2(1): 5-12.

Stroud, C. 1978. "The Concept of Semilingualism". Working Papers 16. University of Lund: Department of Linguistics.
Stroud, C. and Maria Wingstedt. 1989. "Språklig chauvinism?" *Invandrare & Minoriteter*, 16.
Sudderuddin, K. I. (ed.) 1985. *Singapore 1985*. Singapore: Information Division, Ministry of Communication and Information.
Swain, M. and S. Lapkin. 1982. *Evaluating Bilingual Education: A Canadian Case Study*. Clevedon: Multilingual Matters.
Tabouret-Keller, A. 1968. "Social Factors of Language Maintenance and Language shift". In J. Fishman, C. Ferguson, and J. DasGupta (eds.), *Language Problems of Developing Nations*. New York: Wiley.
Tay, Mary W.J. 1983. *Trends in Language, Literacy and Education in Singapore*. Census Monograph 2. Singapore: Department of Education.
Taylor, Philip B. 1984. "Pedagogy, Politics and Bilingual Teaching: The Catalan Case". Paper presented at the Annual Meeting of the Comparative an International Education Society, University of Houston.
Thomason, S. 1982. "Historical Linguistics". Unpublished manuscript.
Thomason, S. and T. Kaufman. 1988. *Language Contact, Creolization, and Genetic Linguistics*. Berkeley: University of California Press.
Thompson, R. M. 1974. "Mexican American Language Loyalty and the Validity of the 1970 Census", *International Journal of the Sociology of Language* 2:6-18.
Tingbjörn, G. 1981. "Ämnesanalys i svenska som främmande språk". MS. Commission on Upper Secondary Education.
Tollefson, J. W. 1991. *Planning Language, Planning Inequality*. New York: Longman.
Tosi, A. 1984. *Immigration and Bilingual Education: A Case Study of Movement of Population, Language Change and Education within the EEC*. Oxford: Pergamon Press.
Toukomaa, P., and Skutnabb-Kangas, T. 1977. *The Intensive Teaching of the Mother Tongue to Migrant Children at Pre-School Age*. University of Tampere, Sociology.
Toukomaa, P., and Lasonen, K. 1979. *On the Literacy of Finnish Immigrant Pupils in Sweden*. University of Jyväskylä.
Touraine, A. 1985. "Sociological Intervention and the Internal Dynamics of the Occitanist Movement". In E. A. Tiryakian and R. Rogowski (eds.), *New Nationalisms of the Developed West*. Boston: Allen and Unwin.
Tovey, H. 1988. "The State of the Irish Language: the Role of Bord na Gaeilge", *International Journal of Sociology of Language* 70:53-68.
Trankell, A. 1974. "Om svenskarnas förhållningssätt och inställning till invandrarna", *Invandrarutredningen* 4. Stockholm: Swedish Government Official Reports.

Trankell, A. 1981. "Fördomar och diskriminering". *Att leva med mångfalden.* Stockholm: Liber.
Trueta, J. 1946. *The Spirit of Catalonia.* London: Oxford University Press.
UNESCO. 1952. Memorandum on the anti-catalan policy of General Franco's government submitted to the delegates of the seventh assembly of UNESCO. Paris, 1952.
UNESCO. 1984. "Mother Tongue and Educational Attainment", *Prospects* 14:1.
Vallverdú, F. 1973. *El fet lingüístic com a fet social.* Barcelona: Edicions 62.
Vallverdú, F. 1981. *El conflicto lingüístico en Cataluña: Historia y presente.* Barcelona: Ediciones Península.
van den Berghe, P. L. 1968. "Language and 'Nationalism' in South Africa." In J. A. Fishman, C. A. Ferguson, and J. DasGupta (eds.), *Language Problems in Developing Nations.* New York: Wiley.
van den Berghe, P. L. 1970. *Race and Ethnicity: Essays in Comparative Sociology.* New York: Basic Books.
van der Planck, P. H. 1972. "The Linguistic Assimilation of Language Minorities in Europe", *La Monda Linguo-Problemo* 4:96-105.
Veltman, C. 1983. *Language Shift in the United States.* Berlin: Mouton.
Verdoodt, A. 1972. "The Differential Impact of Immigrant French Speakers on Indigenous German Speakers: A Case Study in the Light of Two Theories". In J. A. Fishman (ed.), *Advances in the Sociology of Language,* Vol. 2. The Hague: Mouton.
Verdoodt, A. (ed.) 1978. "Belgium", *International Journal of the Sociology of Language* 15: 5-8
von Gleich, V. 1989. *Educación Primaria Bilingüe Intercultural en América Latina.* Rossdorf, Germany: Deutsche Gesellschaft für Technische Zusammenarbeit.
Wande, E. 1977. "Hansegård är ensidig", *Invandrare och Minoriteter* 3/4:44-51.
Wennerström, G. 1967. *Språklig anpassning och studieframgång hos barn till utländska föräldrare.* Stockholm: Department for Educational Research, Institute of Education.
Westin, C. 1981. "Ideologi och etniskt oberoende. Om några försök att anordna arbete åt en etnisk minoritetsgrupp". *Att leva med mångfalden.* Stockholm: Publica/Liber.
Whiteley, W. 1969. *Swahili—the Rise of a National Language.* London: Methuen.
Whiteley, W. H. W. 1971. *Language Use and Social Change.* London: Oxford University Press.
Whiteley, W. H. (ed.) 1974. *Language in Kenya.* Nairobi: Oxford University Press.
Widgren, J. 1981. "Den andra generationen invandrare: Europas framtidsfråga." Paper delivered in Lissabon, ILO seminary, May 1981.

Williams, C. H. (ed.) 1988. *Language in Geographic Context*. Clevedon, Avon: Multilingual Matters.

Woolard, K. A. 1983. "The Politics of Language and Ethnicity in Barcelona, Spain." Unpublished doctoral dissertation, Department of Anthropology, University of California, Berkeley.

Woolard, K. A. 1984. "A Formal Measure of Language Attitudes in Barcelona: a Note from Work in Progress", *International Journal of the Sociology of Language* 47:63-71.

Woolard, K. A. 1986. "The Crisis in the Concept of Identity". In G.W. McDonogh (ed.), *Conflict in Catalonia: Images of Urban Society*. Gainesville: University of Florida Press.

Woolard, K. A. 1989. *Double Talk: Bilingualism and the Politics of Ethnicity in Catalonia*. Stanford: Stanford Unversity Press.

Author Index

A
Abd al-Latif Sharara 34
Abdulaziz 61
Abel 48, 51, 54, 55
Alba 16, 36
Albert 21
Albo 19
Anderson 71
Arnberg 67

B
Baetens Beardsmore 18
Baker 18, 21
Barth ix, 20, 32, 68, 69
Bauman 10
Bec 50
Bennett 28, 29, 33
Benton 102
Blanc 21
Brochetti 38
Brudner 5, 13, 20, 47, 58, 86, 108

C
Carillo 16, 17
Castile 10
Cazden 18, 38
Center for Applied Linguistics 18
Chen 91
Churchill 18
Cohen 18
Connerty 91
Conrad 9

Cooper 9
Cottam 34
Crawford 38
Crewe 59
Cummins 18, 21
Curry 47

D
Dalto 10
Deutsch 26
Dorian 9, 47
Douhan 31
Dressler 9

E
Eckert 13, 49, 50, 51, 55
Edwards 80, 84, 85
Ekstrand 70
Ekvall 71
Elazar 28, 60
Ellis 92
Engle 7
Escobar 64

F
Fase 10, 28
Fasold 81
Ferguson 21, 85
Fishman 5, 9, 26, 27, 43, 45, 47, 91
Foster 18
Friedman 28, 60

G
Gal 10, 13
Garcia 18
Giner 56, 57
Glazer 24, 27
Glinert 8
Gopinathan 104
Gordon 15, 49, 51
Grandguillaume 21
Grimshaw 44
Grosjean 21
Gunter 57
Gunther 48, 53

H
Hamers 21
Hansegård 70, 71
Hartford 18
Haugen 56, 65
Hayakawa 38
Heath 5, 65
Hill 61
Hilmerson 71
Hindley 9
Hinnebusch 61
Holm 17
Hornberger 65
Hornby 21
Hyltenstam 67, 71, 74

J
Jaspaert 10, 28
Jelonek 73
Jernudd 5
Johnston 10

K
Kabir 22
Kaufman 19

Kirsch ix
Kloss 65
Kohn 29, 34, 37, 57
Kroon 10, 28
Kuhn 28
Kushner 10
Kuusinen 69

L
Lafont 49
Laitner 26
Lambert 18, 21
Lapkin 18
Laprade 65
Lasonen 69
Levy 20
Lieberson 10, 12, 18, 47
Liljegren 70, 72
Loman 71
Lopez 15

M
mac a'Ghobhainn 92
Mackey 18, 21
Macnamara 80, 81
Mannheim 6
Martin-Jones 71
McConnell 18, 65
McNair 52, 53
Miracle 21
Moynihan 27

N
Nahir 5, 7, 93, 94, 95
Nystål 71

O
O'Barr 61
Obler 21
Öhman 71

Author Index

Oriol 37
Ornstein 18

P
Patch 6, 66
Paulston, C.B. 7, 18, 68, 101
Paulston, R.G. 11, 29
Petersen 72, 73
Philips 19
Pi-Sunyer 52, 55, 58
Polome 61
Posner 49, 51

R
Read 53
Riesman 27
Rodriguez 16, 17
Romaine 21, 71
Rönmark 71
Rosier 17
Rossinyol ix
Royce 30, 36
Rubin 21

S
Sachs 23
Särkelä 69
Schermerhorn 10, 13, 14, 21, 33, 108
Schlieben-Lange 13, 50
Scotton 60
Shabad 48, 53, 57
Shafer 33, 34, 76, 102
Siguan 52, 53, 54, 101
Similä 70
Sithole 34
Sjöberg 71
Skutnabb-Kangas 69
Snow 18, 38

Spicer 10
Spolsky 17, 18, 102
Stolt 71
Stroud 71
Sudderuddin 103
Swain 18, 21

T
Tay 104
Taylor 53
Thomason 19, 93
Thompson 12, 18, 35
Tingbjörn 72
Tosi 18
Toukomaa 69
Touraine 56
Trankell 68
Tucker 18

V
Valdman 18
Vallverdu 53
van den Berghe 27
Veltman 47
de Vries 18

W
Wande 71
Wennerström 72
Westin 68
White 86
Whiteley 61, 62
Widgren 72
Wikström 71
Wingstedt 71
Wirth 14
Wodak-Leodolter 9
Woolard 55, 56

Subject Index

A
access to the second language (L2) 17
alphabet 3, 5, 26
annexation 10, 11, 14
assimilate 27, 33, 103
assimilation 13, 14, 15, 16, 17, 28, 31, 37, 38, 57, 68, 72, 73, 74, 75, 84
attitudes 94

B
bilingual 12, 13, 23, 36, 81, 82, 86
bilingual education 6, 9, 16, 17, 18, 70, 75, 104, 107, 108
bilingualism 3, 7, 11, 12, 13, 19, 21, 38, 53, 76, 77, 85, 90, 104
boundary maintenance 20, 33, 70

C
choice of medium of instruction 76
choice of national language 76
clans 26
colonization 11, 14
communicative competence 19, 84
conflict perspective 28
contact situation 10
corpus planning 79, 97, 99, 101, 108

D
degree of control 14
degree of enclosure 14, 21

degree of social enclosure 33
diglossic 21
domains 92, 97, 100

E
education 60
educational policies 25
endogamy 16, 24
equilibrium theory 28
ethnic boundaries 32, 70, 76, 84
ethnic boundary maintenance 45
ethnic identity 90
ethnic movement 75, 87, 108
ethnic movements 45, 79
ethnic nationalism 45, 76, 87, 108
ethnicity x, 4, 22, 25-40, 45, 46, 47, 55, 58, 60, 69, 71, 75, 79, 87, 108
exogamy 13, 17, 18, 31, 63, 83, 102

G
geographic nationalism x, 45, 57, 58, 76, 77, 87, 108, 109
group bilingualism 83

H
home language education 6

I
immigrant 75
immigrant groups 12
immigration 71

incentive 20
incorporation 15

L
language 74
language attitudes 21, 60, 86
language choice 5
language death 9, 10, 47, 51, 58, 81, 91, 92, 93, 102, 106
language loyalty 22, 44
language maintenance ix, 3, 4, 7, 9-24, 28, 31, 32, 35, 39, 43, 44, 45, 46, 47-58, 69, 76, 79-90, 91, 102, 107, 108
language planning 4, 5-8, 25, 39, 62, 79-90, 91-106
language policies 3, 4, 5-8, 46, 73, 75, 76, 77
language problems 3, 5-8, 27, 29, 39
language regenesis 91-106
language reversal 91-106
language revitalization 79-90, 91-106
language revival 91-106
language shift 3, 7, 9-24, 31, 33, 35, 43, 44, 47-58, 68, 75, 79-90, 107
language spread 9, 10
languages 92
lingua franca 4, 9, 44, 61, 63, 94
LWC 4, 9, 18, 38, 95

M
maintain 74
maintain a language 75
maintenance 26
media of instruction 3, 5, 6, 7, 15, 60, 61, 62, 69, 104
migrant group 11
migration 14, 53, 64, 66, 67, 69, 70, 73, 83, 93, 94
militancy 14
militant 32

mobilization 23, 25, 47, 87, 106, 108
mobilize 89
mother tongue education 6

N
national language 5, 15, 18, 20, 22
national or official language 3
nationalism 4, 23, 25-40, 47, 57, 63, 65, 69, 70, 75, 76, 77, 79, 86, 87, 90, 93, 95, 96, 98, 99, 101

O
origin of the contact situation 10-12, 12, 14

P
pan-dialectal 49
pan-movements 26
paradigm shift 28
pluralism 14

R
rate of shift 15, 19, 24, 75
revival 5, 7, 91

S
secessionist 14
semilingualism 70, 71
shift 4, 38, 39, 45, 46, 63, 70, 74, 76, 77, 91, 108
Status planning 79
status planning 99, 109

T
territorial 47, 49
territorially 37
territory 35, 37, 56, 76, 100
tribe 26, 27, 63

V
Voluntary migration 10, 75

In the series STUDIES IN BILINGUALISM (SiBil) the following titles have been published and will be published during 1994:
1. FASE, Willem, Koen JASPAERT and Sjaak KROON (eds): *Maintenance and Loss of Minority Languages*. Amsterdam/Philadelphia, 1992.
2. BOT, Kees de, Ralph B. GINSBERG and Claire KRAMSCH (eds): *Foreign Language Research in Cross-Cultural Perspective*. Amsterdam/Philadelphia, 1991.
3. DÖPKE, Susan: *One Parent — One Language: An Interactional Approach*. Amsterdam/Philadelphia, 1992.
4. PAULSTON, Christina Bratt: *Linguistic Minorities in Multilingual Settings. Implications for language policies*. Amsterdam/Philadelphia, 1994.
5. KLEIN, Wolfgang and Clive PERDUE: *Utterance Structure (Developing Grammars Again)*. Amsterdam/Philadelphia, 1992.
6. SCHREUDER, Robert and Bert WELTENS: *The Bilingual Lexicon*. Amsterdam/Philadelphia, 1993.
7. DIETRICH, Rainer, Wolfgang KLEIN and Colette NOYAU: *The Acquisition of Temporality in a Second Language*. Amsterdam/Philadelphia, n.y.p.
8. DAVIS, Kathryn Anne: *Language Planning in Multilingual Contexts. Policies, communities, and schools in Luxembourg*. Amsterdam/Philadelphia, 1994.